Bill Boyd
1906 - 1997

This text is dedicated to the memory of Bill Boyd, card-room manager of the Golden Nugget for 36 years. Due to his diligent efforts and high level of integrity, poker left the smokey back rooms of yesterday and entered today's modern era. Through his efforts, a career as a professional poker dealer became an occupation well worth pursuing.

His values set the standard for the industry.

Table of Contents

Foreword

by Jim Albrecht
World Series of Poker Director

Nothing looks easier than dealing poker when it's done well. In fact, that's part of the appeal of the job. But with this "easy" living goes much responsibility. Poker has many more variations than other casino games, and the rules governing the various poker games are more intricate. Plus, the smallest error or lapse in concentration can cause major problems — thus the need for in-depth training before prospective dealers are introduced to "money" games.

The Professional Poker Dealer's Handbook is an excellent tool for the education of a poker dealer. In fact, it could well become the standard reference book for dealing schools. It is well written, insightful, but most important it makes easy work of a complex subject.

About Dan Paymar

Dan was born and raised in Flint, Michigan. Before turning to a career in the poker industry, Dan spent four years at Michigan Tech, becoming an engineer. His first work in the computer industry was in field service for Bendix Computer, which was bought out by Control Data in 1963. In 1967, Dan moved on to develop a text editing system for Encyclopædia Britannica.

With two other engineers, Dan started Educational Data Systems. Their goal: to write a BASIC language interpreter and disk operating system for the Data General Nova computer to handle up to sixteen users. As far as we know, this was the first time-sharing system ever to run on a minicomputer. When the company began manufacturing its own computers Educational Data Systems became Point 4 Data Corporation.

Always the idea man, Dan then developed an accessory for the Apple-II computer which he sold via his own mail order business and through retail outlets.

In 1989 Dan changed his career direction about 180 degrees and returned to school — to become a poker dealer. That same year, he moved to Las Vegas.

After five years working as a poker dealer, playing some poker, and getting interested in video poker, Dan became an instructor for poker dealers at Casino Gaming School.[1] Not satisfied with the instructional materials then available, the original edition of this book was born. Starting as a booklet of fifty pages, the text evolved as new situations and questions came up in class that were not covered. In 1995, the second edition of the original text, with eighty pages, was published and sold in gaming bookstores.

---

[1]Casino Gaming School is a highly respected dealer's school in Las Vegas.

Other Publications by Dan Paymar

Dan has been playing video poker since 1989 and began analyzing it and writing about it in 1991. Several of his articles have been published in *Card Player,* and he has a regular column in *Blackjack Forum.* Dan and associate newsletter editor Doug Reul are highly respected among both professional and recreational video poker players for their accurate analyses and easy-to-use strategies.

Video Poker — Precision Play™ is a popular book of Dan's that gives the "Precision Play" rules for Jacks-or-Better, Deuces Wild, Joker Wild (Kings-or-Better), and Bonus Deuces. With this book, there is no need to memorize long tables for these games; just follow a few simple rules, and you're playing better than many "experts." A quiz for each of the first three games helps you to hone your skills. The book also covers a variety of progressives and unusual games, the value of comps and slot clubs, bankroll requirements, and how to select games that offer high payback.

Video Poker Times™ is a bi-monthly newsletter invaluable to anyone seeking a profit at video poker.

The Best of Video Poker Times™ *(and more)* is a seventy-six-page book that contains some of the best articles that originally appeared in *Video Poker Times.*

Pocket Sized Strategy Cards (You Can Take It With You) are laminated, shirt pocket size cue cards that are available for most of the "best" video poker machines. Each card provides an accurate hand rank table, and many pros play with a cue card in plain sight.

These products are available directly from Dan Paymar. For information and pricing write to

Dan Paymar
2540 S. Maryland Pkwy, Suite #141
Las Vegas, NV 89109

or visit his web site at www.savenet702.com/video-poker.html.

About Donna Harris

Donna Harris was born and raised in California and came to Las Vegas in 1979 for the World Cup of Darts, which was held at the Sahara Hotel. She was the first female official for this event. Like many Las Vegas visitors, she was fascinated by the prospect of building a career in the casino industry, and in 1980 she returned to Las Vegas to deal blackjack professionally. Her first job was at the Golden Nugget Gambling Hall in downtown Las Vegas.

That same year, after becoming intrigued by the game of poker (which was played directly across the pit from where she dealt), and then playing poker after work, Donna asked to be transferred into the cardroom where the legendary Bill Boyd was the manager. Her initial position was as a "shill dealer" — a dealer who only dealt when the "regular" dealers were out of the lineup — usually to play poker. Her other early job duties included brushing tables, getting fills and player's checks, and "playing poker" as a shill. She dealt poker until 1985.

In 1982 Bill Boyd retired, turning the cardroom over to another legend, Eric Drache. At that time very few women were in poker management and Eric felt that many of his regular customers, who originally played in "smokey back room" type environments, would not respect the decision of a young and inexperienced female floorperson. However, Donna persisted and was given the opportunity to succeed.

In 1998 Donna became the cardroom manager at The Mirage, where you can still find her today. Donna has also held positions in both The World Series of Poker and Grand Prix of Poker tournaments held in Las Vegas. Her experience includes traveling with Poker Cruises International, whose routes to most ports in the Caribbean and Mexico have now been taken over by Card Player Cruises and Classic Poker Cruises. She was also aboard the first "poker cruise" to England on the QE II in 1985, and worked poker tournaments in such exotic locales as Marakesh, Morocco, and Port Vila, Vanuatu.

About Mason Malmuth

Mason Malmuth was born and raised in Coral Gables, Florida. In 1973 he received his B.S. in mathematics from Virginia Tech, and completed their Masters' program in 1975. While working as a mathematical statistician for the United States Census Bureau in 1978, Mason stopped overnight in Las Vegas while driving to his new assignment in California. He was immediately fascinated by the games, and gambling became his major interest.

After arriving in California he discovered that poker was legal and began playing in some of the public cardrooms, as well as taking periodic trips to Las Vegas where he would play both poker and blackjack. In 1981 he went to work for the Northrop Corporation as a mathematician and moved to Los Angeles where he could conveniently pursue his interest in poker in the large public cardrooms in Gardena, Bell Gardens, and Commerce.

In 1983 his first article "Card Domination — The Ultimate Blackjack Weapon" was published in *Gambling Times* magazine. By 1987 he had left his job with the Northrop Corporation to begin a career as both a full-time gambler and a gambling writer. He has had over five hundred articles published in various magazines and is the author and/or co-author of thirteen books. These include *Gambling Theory and Other Topics,* in which he sets out to demonstrate why only a small number of people are highly successful at gambling. In this book he also introduces the reader to the concept of "non-self-weighting strategies" and explains why successful gambling is actually a balance of luck and skill. Other books he has co-authored are *Gambling for a Living* and *Hold 'em Poker For Advanced Players,* written with David Sklansky, and *Seven-Card Stud For Advanced Players* written with David Sklansky and Ray Zee. The two "advanced" books are considered the definitive works on these games.

His company Two Plus Two Publishing has sold over 200,000 books and currently has twenty titles to its credit. These books are recognized as the best in their field and are thoroughly studied by those individuals who take gambling seriously. For more information about Two Plus Two Publishing, visit their web sit at www.twoplustwo.com.

Other Books by Mason Malmth

Gambling Theory and Other Topics
Poker Essays
Poker Essays, Volume II
Blackjack Essays
Winning Concepts in Draw and Lowball

Other Books with Mason Malmuth

Hold 'em Poker For Advanced Players by David Sklansky and Mason Malmuth
Seven-Card Stud For Advanced Players by David Sklansky, Mason Malmuth, and Ray Zee
Gambling for a Living by David Sklansky and Mason Malmuth

Booklets with Mason Malmuth

Fundamentals of Craps by Mason Malmuth and Lynne Loomis
Fundamentals of Poker by Mason Malmuth and Lynne Loomis
Fundamentals of "21" by Mason Malmuth and Lynne Loomis
Fundamentals of Video Poker by Mason Malmuth and Lynne Loomis

A Note From Two Plus Two

This book has a history. An earlier version of it was originally written and published in 1995 by Dan Paymar and was used as a teaching manual at the Casino Gaming School in Las Vegas, Nevada.

In 1997 Dan approached Two Plus Two Publishing to see if we would be interested in a wider publication of his book. We felt a need definitely existed for such a text in the rapidly expanding poker industry. To this end it was decided that the original text would be rewritten and expanded and that Donna Harris of The Mirage, and Mason Malmuth of Two Plus Two Publishing would lend their time and expertise to the project as well.

After much work involving all three principals we have produced *The Professional Poker Dealer's Handbook*. We consider it must reading for anyone involved in the poker industry and expect this text to set the standard for years to come.

To accompany this book, additional training materials are available if you are a gaming school director or poker instructor: For $25.00 a set of three written tests, the correct answers, scoring method, and a practical evaluation form can be ordered from Dan Paymar. These were developed by Dan over a three-year period while working as a poker dealing instructor. The fee gives you the right to reproduce the forms as they are or to modify them as you see fit for use in one training location.

The tests and evaluations are geared to the suggested course outline in the back of this book. If you are interested in this material contact:

Dan Paymar
2540 S. Maryland Pkwy, Suite #141
Las Vegas, NV 89109
E-mail address: vptimes@wizard.com

Introduction

Poker as an industry has grown at a phenomenal rate during the past few years. It wasn't that long ago that only a few Nevada casinos had small poker rooms merely as an accommodation for their customers. Even in those states where poker was legal, there were generally so many restrictions that the industry was kept artificially small.

Today this has changed. As casino gambling has spread across the United States and Canada, poker has been there right along with it. In fact, poker may now be the fastest growing segment of the casino industry, and it is easy to see why.

As more and more people get greater access to casino gambling, they need a game that is more interesting and has enough appeal to keep them coming back over and over. *Poker is this game.* And, as evidence of this, its growth has been explosive. Today, huge poker rooms spreading all limits and many different types of poker now exist in many locations across the country.

Poker tournaments have kept pace with the growth. The World Series of Poker hosted by Binion's Horseshoe Hotel and Casino in downtown Las Vegas as just one example, attracts thousands of poker enthusiasts every year. It is hard to believe that in 1970 this event began as a small gathering of high-limit players.

However, poker has its problems. As with any industry that grows this fast, there are bound to be some "growing pains." A lack of quality poker dealers is immediately apparent to anyone who either plays poker or works in the industry, and poor poker dealers hurt everyone involved.

Players resent incompetent dealers because they slow the game down by making numerous errors. Poker room management is unhappy with poor dealers because they contribute to poker room problems, help create an adversarial relationship between players and management, and reduce the overall revenue of a cardroom. Competent dealers do not appreciate their incompetent counterparts

1

since they help to put players in a "bad mood," thus reducing all dealer's "tokes."

In the past most dealer problems had been attributed to player abuse. While we recognize that player abuse is a problem — particularly at the higher limits — we also recognize that many players who get out of line do so because they have been upset by incompetent dealing. It's frequently true that they are overreacting, but in many cases there might have been no problem to begin with if the dealer had done his or her job correctly.

As can be seen, a lot needs to be done in this area. Poker is a fascinating game with a great future. But for this future to be optimized the industry and the players must move forward together. That's why we have produced *The Professional Poker Dealer's Handbook*. It is a comprehensive guide that all dealers and cardroom personnel should read. It should also be read by most regular players. But most importantly, it should serve to bridge the gap in an industry that needs good, competent, and most of all, *Professional* dealers.

Finally, we would like to express our appreciation to Paula Cizmar for editing this work. Thanks to her, our ideas are now more clearly stated and thus should be more easily understood. In addition, we wish to thank Dave Clint for his cover design and art work throughout the book.

Dealer's Work Ethic

Each person employed at a casino, or any business for that matter, has a job. A job is a defined set of tasks and duties done by agreement for pay.

Each of us perceives our work differently. Some see it as an occupation, others view it as a career. There is a distinct difference between these two perceptions. An occupation is that which occupies or engages one's time in pursuit of money. A career is one's achievement in a particular profession. The word "profession" is quite significant.

A profession is a body of persons in a particular occupation who require training and skill and whose job requires focus and concentration. A sales clerk, for example, is involved in an occupation requiring only minimal training and skill. A casino dealer, however, must pay constant attention to the game in addition to being well trained. Therefore, a casino dealer is involved in a profession, whereas the sales clerk may not be. Of course there are exceptions to any generalization; some sales positions require a great deal of skill and training, and some poker dealers are very unprofessional.

It is logical that if one is engaged in a profession then that person should be a professional. A professional is one having experience and skill in a specified role — that is, one who is engaged in and worthy of the high standards of their profession. A true professional also continually strives to improve those skills rather than just get by.

It is the responsibility of each casino to definitively set forth the standards of professionalism expected of its dealers. A few casinos provide an ongoing training program to enhance their dealers' skills. These employers constantly monitor progress and evaluate the level of professional skill attained by each dealer.

Unfortunately, many other casinos are very lax in this area. They audition a dealer for initial employment but then ignore the situation when that same dealer gets lazy and sloppy. It is left up to individual shift managers, or even to the dealers themselves, to establish and enforce standards. If you play any of the games, you will notice the difference as you move from one casino to another. Which casino do you prefer to play in? Which dealers get more tokes?

In light of all this, it's clear that those dealers who view their job as just an occupation are not seeing the meaning and full value of their position. This brings us to the purpose of this book. Dealers who adhere to and apply professional standards as outlined herein shall reap maximum benefits. Those who are unable to achieve those professional standards, or who choose not to maintain those standards, shall reap very little.

Accuracy and Technique Come First

Whether practicing or dealing a live game, *always put accuracy and technique before speed.*

The old adage "Practice makes perfect" can be deceptive. As any musician will tell you, practice will result in a flawless performance only if you avoid repeating errors and continue practicing and correcting errors until errors no longer occur.

It would be better to remember that practice makes *permanent*. Practicing incorrectly is not only wasted time, but the poor technique may become a habit, making it even harder to improve. The only way to hone your skills is to practice correct technique.

Rushing only impedes your progress. Practice slowly and accurately. Speed is desirable, but it should be allowed to come naturally through good technique, efficiency, and experience.

Part
1
Objectives

Objectives

Introduction

If you as a poker dealer know and understand everyone's objectives and how management views those objectives, then you will better realize how important your individual role is — and how it fits into the scheme of a successful operation. You must keep in mind that a successful poker room is a team effort.

You, the poker dealer, are a very important member of this team. You must be able to work successfully with your fellow dealers, the other cardroom personnel, and the players to whom you deal to. You must also keep in mind the objectives of the casino, the cardroom, and your customers. But most important of all, you must pay strict attention to the game at hand and do your job quietly and efficiently.

Many dealers claim their job is a difficult one. Most players feel that anyone can be a competent dealer. We recognize that becoming a competent and efficient dealer is not easy. However, we do believe that with the proper attitude and effort there is no excuse for not becoming a *professional*. In this way, a dealer's job can be a rewarding one.

Casino Objectives

The sole and exclusive reason that any business, including a casino, exists is to derive a profit. There is no greed in this. It's a matter of reality in our economic system, and it's what made the United States a great financial power.

As in any business, the casino attains the profit objective by servicing the lifeblood of its business, the customer. Without sufficient customers, a profit could not be realized, and there would be no need for the casino or its employees. The casino serves the customers by providing them with the facilities and ingredients necessary for them to attain their individual objectives. Satisfied customers will return to play again, and they will tell their friends.

It's not always easy to satisfy customers in a poker room. The game can be frustrating at times, and no one likes to lose. But in poker there must be losers, so at times frustration will abound.

Given these facts, it is important that poker games be well run in all aspects. This will help assure that customers will have an enjoyable cardroom experience; which will make them more inclined to return again. A key ingredient to this is the dealer: Unless the dealer does his job, well run poker games cannot occur.

Customer Objectives

Basically, the objectives of the customer condense to social enjoyment, recreation, and in the case of poker, the opportunity to pursue a profit.

Customers can achieve their objectives through the facilities provided by the casino coupled with special ingredients provided by the employees — including a congenial and harmonious atmosphere in which enjoyment is a key factor and a standardized, smooth-running, and mechanically efficient game that offers fast-paced play and a promise of fair treatment.

Some customers come to poker rooms for entertainment, some come to win (and some come for both). But one thing is certain. A fast-paced, well-run poker game will satisfy almost all players.

Throughout this book we will stress the idea of *quiet and efficient* dealing. There is a reason for this, and that reason is that this is precisely the type of poker dealer that almost all poker players prefer. That is, it's what the customer wants and what they have a right to expect.

Dealer Objectives

Casino dealers obviously seek to derive an income to support themselves and their families. Hopefully, they also want to save for their futures, be a part of something they can take pride in, and feel a sense of achievement. A dealer can attain these objectives by constantly striving for excellence on the job, by working for the benefit of the whole in a cohesive team effort with the casino and poker room to assist customers in attaining their goals. Tokes (tips) are the lifeblood of a dealer, and a dealer receives the most tokes when he or she serves the customers' objectives as efficiently as possible.

Notice that we did not use the word "friendly." While we agree that dealers should always be polite and pleasant, we need to stress that dealers need to be non-talkative and extremely focused on the game. Put another way, *there should be no extraneous talking in the box.* Be polite, but do not engage in conversations. Dealers who talk are more prone to errors — which sometimes erupt into big commotions.

Those dealers who deal the most hands virtually error free are the ones who make the most money. A fast-paced poker game is the type players like the best and the ones in which they'll tip the most. *Always remember this.* When you are in the box, this should be your objective.

Part
2
General Information

General Information

Introduction

In this chapter, we'll talk about typical cardrooms and poker in general as it is played in a casino environment. Although some of this information applies primarily to Nevada casinos, most of it applies wherever poker is played in public cardrooms

Many of the procedures described in this chapter require a floorperson's decision, so don't assume that as a dealer you should always go ahead and do as it says here on your own. A later chapter, "Dealer Information," will outline when a floorperson must be called.[2] If you encounter a term you don't understand, refer to the glossary in the back of this handbook.

Virtually everyone has played a little poker at one time or another, but casino poker is very different from the home game variety. Please pay close attention to the description of casino poker that is provided. This section will help assure that your transition into the casino environment is a smooth one.

---

[2]One area of concern is dealers who try to make rulings when they are in the box. In many cases, trying to make a ruling, even if you are absolutely sure what the floorperson's decision will be, will only make the problem worse. This is because only the floorperson has the authority to make a decision final.

Nevada Casino Cardrooms

In Nevada casinos, poker is usually separate from the pit games, slots, and other departments. In casinos with only one or two tables, however, poker may be part of the pit games department. In some cases, other card games such as pan (panguingue), pai gow poker, Caribbean Stud™ and Let It Ride™ might be part of the cardroom. But generally poker rooms only spread poker, and a poker room is frequently its own unique environment inside the casino.

Unlike most other casino games, the house does not take part in the action in a poker game. The dealer does not receive a hand, and wagers are made only between players. The casino makes its profit by taking a percentage "rake" from each pot, a per-hand collection, or a time collection usually each half hour. In exchange for this rake or collection, the casino provides an air conditioned room, all the necessary equipment, and frequently complimentary drinks. Comped meals are also earned by the players. Also, the casino environment assures security. Most importantly, the players (rightfully) expect the casino to provide a professional dealer who is trained to run the game efficiently. In just a short time you can be that professional dealer.

Cardrooms in Other States

Many states now allow legal poker. There may not be any blackjack or craps games, other pit games, or slot machines in the casinos. In some jurisdictions, particularly California, the rake and button are handled differently. However, the game of poker is basically the same everywhere, and for the most part the techniques and procedures described herein apply. Probably the biggest difference is that in California lowball draw is also played. This game is actually a holdover from an earlier era where only forms of draw poker were legal.[3] But it is quickly dying out as most players prefer stud or hold 'em because of the greater amount of action these games provide.

Even though there may be differences in the way a cardroom operates outside of Nevada as we have stated, poker is still poker. That is, the players look forward to and expect the dealer to perform his or her job in a professional manner.

---

[3] Actually, the law didn't change. In California, the legal status of gambling is based upon an antique (ca. 1895) law that states only which games are *not* allowed. Included in the prohibited games are blackjack, faro, and "stud horse poker," which for many years the Attorney General defined to include all forms of stud poker — and even ruled that Texas hold 'em was a form of stud poker. Finally the card casinos sued to be allowed to spread a form of draw poker that mimicked some aspects of hold 'em. The court surprised everyone and decided that all forms of seven-card poker should be legal.

Casino Poker

Since dealer information is presented separately in a later chapter, most of the following is useful for players as well as dealers.

The information included here is not game or cardroom specific. Since rules and policies vary from jurisdiction to jurisdiction and from casino to casino, these generalities are subject to change. Be sure to check with the manager of the cardroom where you will be playing or working if there are any questions.

Casino poker is played with a standard fifty-two-card deck. Most cardrooms use the narrow "bridge size" plastic cards, which are much easier to handle than the wide paper cards commonly used in home poker games and casino pit games. A spare deck is kept in the dealer's rack so that the deck can be changed without having to call a floorperson. If lowball draw is offered the joker may be added to the deck, but these games are rare outside California. If you expect to be dealing in a major tournament or in a state where these games are common, ask the instructor or tournament director for additional information.

At the time of this writing, a coordinated effort between several cardrooms is underway to standardize many of the rules. However, until this comes about there will be some differences between cardrooms about how poker should be played and controlled. The best we can do here is list the most common rules along with some variations that you might encounter. Wherever you play, always feel free to ask questions.

Some rules and procedures apply in most public cardrooms, regardless of the form of poker. Remember, however, that a particular cardroom's rules and policies always take precedence over these generalities, and a floorperson's decision is final.

1. Players must protect their own hands at all times. This may be the most important rule in all of poker. A hand *may* be declared "dead" if even one card touches the muck or if another player's card touches a hand that is not protected. A hand may be protected by the player placing a chip or other object on top of the cards or by holding on to the cards. Although the dealer should be aware of only mucking discarded hands, a player who fails to take reasonable means to protect his or her hand usually has no recourse if the hand becomes fouled or if the dealer accidentally collects an unprotected hand.

While it is not necessary for the winner of a pot to show the hand if there were no callers, it is suggested that the player protect the winning hand until the dealer is actually pushing the pot to him. The dealer should not ask the player to relinquish the winning hand before pushing the pot.

2. One player to a hand. Neither the dealer, another player, nor anyone else may assist a player in any way during the play of a hand. This prohibition includes but is not limited to giving advice, reminding a player about exposed cards, or turning up the player's cards at the showdown. However, it is permissible in most cardrooms for another person to watch (or "sweat") someone in a game.[4] But the rule of one person to a hand still applies.

3. Only English may be spoken. Since English is the main language used in the United States only English may be spoken by any player or observer during play of a hand, and anything said to or by a player with a live hand must be loud enough for other players to hear. This is a logical extension of the "one player to a hand" rule. How would you know if players were being helped or were passing information to each other if they were whispering or were speaking a language that you and the others didn't understand?

---

[4]Occasionally someone will play who, because of a handicap, requires assistance of another person. This is usually accepted by the other players, and the person giving assistance does not have any input in the actual strategy employed. He only follows instructions.

4. Cards must remain in sight. All players' cards must be kept in view so that the dealer and other players can see who has a hand. This will help assure that all players act in turn. Those players who stack their chips in an effort to hide their cards so that they can discover the action behind them should be informed (by the floorperson) that this will not be tolerated.

5. All cards must be kept above the table. The player is not allowed to play the cards "close to the vest" unless seated close enough so that the cards are not taken past the edge of the table. At the floorperson's discretion, a player's hand may be declared dead if the cards are taken out of sight.

6. The player is responsible to turn up his cards. All a player's cards must be turned up *by that player* in order to be considered in the showdown. The hand is considered unreadable until all cards are shown. It is not necessary to show the hand, however, if the win is by default because all competing hands have been discarded.

7. Cards speak. If all a player's cards are turned face up by the player then the cards themselves determine the value of the hand regardless of how it might have been called, and the highest ranking hand wins the pot. Anyone may point out that a hand is not as good or is actually better than it was called. It is the dealer's responsibility to read the hand correctly and push the pot to the player having the best live hand. (This does *not* take precedence over rule 1.)

8. Verbal declarations may be binding. Verbal bets or raises may be binding if it causes anyone else to act on their hand. At management's discretion, any player who is deliberately miscalling his hand — or doing some other unethical act that could cause other players to act prematurely on their hand, may risk forfeiting the pot. In addition, such players should be warned that any future actions of this type could result in a more severe penalty.

9. The final decision of the winning hand is always based on exactly five cards. If, for example, two players each have a nine-high straight, they split the pot. The sixth or seventh cards are never considered as kickers. There is no such hand as three pair. (In split-pot games it is not necessary to use the *same* five cards for high and low.)

10. Suit has no significance. In poker all suits are considered equal. The only exception is to determine the bring-in hand in stud where the lowest card by suit, using bridge suits — clubs, diamonds, hearts, and spades — is required to initiate the action. (Notice that the suits are in alphabetical order.)

11. When there is no action, the hands are shown down in order. If everyone hesitates showing their hands after completion of all action, then the players are obligated to show their hands in the order by which they had the option to bet. (There are a small number of cardrooms, mostly in Europe, that require the person who initiated the last action — bet or raise on a previous street — to show first.)

12. Every game has a minimum buy-in. When entering a game, a new player must put money on the table at least equal to the specified buy-in for that game. The buy-in is typically five times the maximum bet, but it is determined by house policy. Also in many rooms only chips play; or, bills smaller than $100 are not allowed. If that is the case, all money (except for $100 bills where appropriate) will need to be converted into chips.

13. Check and raise is permitted. Unless specifically prohibited, a player is allowed to check his hand and then raise if someone else bets. This is often denounced as "sandbagging" in home games, but is an accepted practice in public cardrooms.

14. Declaring all-in. A player may declare himself all-in when he does not have enough money on the table to cover a bet. This qualifies the player to contend for the pot up to the amount matched, and any further action goes into a side pot to be contested between the other active players. (See "Table Stakes" and "Side Pot Procedures" on pages 26 and 149 respectively for more information.) Many cardrooms now have a "minimum size chip" declaration. This means that a player can declare all-in only in increments of the value of this chip. For example, in a $10-$20 game, where $5 chips are common, if a player has $7 left he can only be all-in for $5.

15. Playing behind. A player may "play behind" (begin with no money on the table) only if money has been given to a cardroom employee for the purpose of getting chips.

16. Maximum amount to bet. A bet and three raises are allowed for each betting round in most cardrooms, although some rooms allow four or even five raises. We recommend that a bet and four raises be the standard. With only three raises some players are very quick to "cap" the betting, thus producing a game that frequently plays larger than if four raises are allowed.

17. What constitutes a bet. Only a full bet or raise, or half or more of a full bet if going all-in, constitutes a bet or raise in a structured-limit game. Anything less than half a bet, or any increase by less than half the bet or last raise, is considered to be action only, and completing such a bet is counted as the actual bet or raise. For example, suppose the bet is $20 and a player goes all-in for $5. The next player can either fold, call the $5, or complete the bet to $20. He cannot raise to $25.

If a player goes all-in for half or more of a full bet or raise in a structured-limit game, and there are other players yet to act, this bet is considered to be a full bet. The next player can fold, call the bet, or raise by the amount of the limit. For example, suppose the bet is $20 and a player goes all-in for $15. The next player can either fold, call the $15, or raise to $35. He cannot just complete the bet to $20.

18. Head-up action. There is no limit to the number of raises when only two active players remain at the beginning of a betting round. This is because either player can end the raising by simply calling. In some rooms, the number of raises becomes unlimited as soon as the action is down to two players even if there were more active players at the beginning of that round provided the cap had not been reached while the pot was still multihanded.

19. String bets. String bets or raises are not allowed. A player must either put the full amount of money out at one time or announce the intended action before releasing any money. The two move "I call... and raise..." shown in the movies is not allowed because it may be used to gain additional information about hand strengths (usually of players who have not yet acted).

20. Splashing the pot. Players must not "splash the pot" (put chips directly into the pot). This makes it difficult for the other players to see exactly how much that player put in. Each player should place his or her bets directly in front of the seat position. If a player spreads chips on the table, the dealer should reposition the chips in front of the player. If a player splashes the pot, the dealer should politely explain this rule and be prepared to interpose with his hand the next time it is that player's turn to act.

21. Large chips. A single chip or a bill that is larger than the bet is just a call unless that player announces "raise" before it hits the table — a tie is a call.

22. Boxed cards. A card found to be face up in the deck (a "boxed card") is treated as a piece of paper. A card being treated as a piece of paper is shown and announced to all players and mucked, and the next card immediately replaces it.

23. Foreign cards. Any card that is foreign to the deck, such as a duplicate card or a card with a different color back, immediately fouls the deck, and all monies are returned to all players *who* *received cards at the beginning of that hand.* A joker dealt face up in a game that does not use a joker is treated like a boxed card and the next card immediately replaces it. A joker dealt face down is replaced by the top card of the deck after everyone has received their down cards. If a player knowingly tries to win the pot with a fouled deck then he has a dead hand and forfeits all rights to the pot and all monies involved.

24. Asking to be dealt in. If a player posts a blind, antes, and/or asks to be dealt in, but is not at the table when it is time to act on his hand, he forfeits any such money including any forced entry bet. However, the hand remains live until such time as there is a need to call or fold, whereupon the hand will be mucked. If the player returns before the hand is mucked, he may play it.

25. Significant action. In most cardrooms, significant action is defined as two or more players acting on their hands in turn. (Note: Action includes both checking and folding, as well as betting.)

26. Incorrect number of cards. If a player does not have the correct number of cards on the deal, and there has been no action, it is a misdeal. If there has been significant action then that player's hand is declared dead and he loses any ante or blinds that he may have posted. Remember, it is the player's responsibility to protect his or her own hand — and this includes making sure he or she was dealt the proper number of cards.

27. Cards off the table. A card accidentally dealt off the table is usually treated as an exposed card. However, a card dropped off the table by a player will not be replaced and may cause the hand to be declared dead. (The floorperson will make the decision.)

28. Splitting pots. All hands must be played to completion. The dealer can split a pot only when the hands are tied or if the form of poker being played is high-low split. An exception may be if no one calls the blinds, the blinds may agree to just take them back.[5] The splitting of pots among players is generally only allowed in high-stakes games. (Note: When allowed, the dealer should push the pot to one of the players and the player will split it.)

29. Eight-or-better. An eight or better is required to qualify for low in a high-low split game unless a specific posting of no qualifier is made. "Eight-or-better" means five cards of different ranks eight or lower. (An ace is the lowest card.)

30. Straddle bets. In most games with blinds, the first player after the blinds may post a "straddle" bet, usually twice the amount of the big blind before any cards have been dealt. The "straddle" is live, giving that player the last option to check or raise. (Note: In most rooms this does not affect the cap and is treated as the first raise.)

31. Burning a card. After each round of betting, and before the next round of cards is dealt, lightly tap the table to indicate to the players that you are about to deal. You will then "burn" the top card from the deck, placing it under the edge of the pot where it will remain (with the other burns) until the pot is pushed. This is done in case there is some irregularity on the deal and "clean" cards are needed. (Burn cards also protect the top of the deck and the game from exposed cards. They are also used to complete a hand where necessary.)

32. Any player can see a called hand. Often a player will discard his hand when another player shows a better hand at the showdown. However, any active player at the table may request to see all called hands before the cards are thrown into the muck. (In some rooms, only the players that called the last bet have the option to ask to see a discarded hand.) When a request is made, the dealer should tap the hand face down on the muck to kill it, then turn it up. However,

---

[5]Though accepted, we feel that chopping the blinds is bad for the game.

in a few rooms a folded hand that has called all bets is *not* killed on the muck before it is shown *if it was the presumed winner who asked to see it;* this way the player that asks runs the risk that the discarded hand could turn out to be the winner.

33. Show one, show all. If a player shows his hand to another player then, upon request by any other player, he must show it to all players. If the betting action is not finished, and a hand is shown to a player who still has a live hand, then the shown hand must be shown to the entire table immediately. If it is shown to a player who has already folded then it is not shown to the rest of the table until after the action is finished. If a player bets, and all others fold, and he shows his hand to any other player, then the hand must be shown to the entire table.

34. Only the dealer makes change. Players may not make change for their bets from the pot. The dealer will make change, sometimes immediately and sometimes when all action on the betting round has been completed. The exception is that a player is generally allowed to make change from his own earlier bet for the current betting round if it is still in front of him.

35. The dealer pushes the pot. The winner of a hand should not reach for the pot. The dealer will push the pot to the winner.

36. Floorperson's decision. In case of any argument or questionable circumstances, a floorperson must be called to make a decision. As the dealer, you never make a decision even though you may know the correct ruling. All decisions by the floorperson are final.

37. Regarding decisions. The dealer is responsible for imparting the facts concerning the immediate problems only. Impressions and opinions are both unnecessary and destructive to the decision-making process. (Note: Always call your table number when calling for a decision.)

Table Stakes

All games are table stakes. That is, only the money, and all of the money, that a player has on the table at the beginning of a hand will play during that hand.

As a result of this rule:

1. A player may not be put at risk for more money than he has voluntarily put on the table.
2. A player cannot be forced out of a pot because he does not have enough money to call all bets.
3. A player may not take advantage of a strong hand by putting more money on the table after receiving cards.
4. If there has been a bet, a player may not hold back any money that was on the table at the beginning of a hand except by folding.
5. A player may not take money off the table until leaving the game. (Exceptions include tokes to the dealer and cocktail server.)

When a player runs out of money during the play of a hand but wants to stay in the hand, he declares "all-in," thus becoming eligible to compete for money in the pot up to that point.

A player who runs out of money can win only the main pot. A side pot is created so that the remaining players can still bet and win both, assuming they have the best hand. All the bets that have been matched by the all-in player go into the main pot, and all further action goes into the side pot to be contested only between players that are still active.

If another player goes all-in, he is eligible to win the main pot and the first side pot, and the dealer will start another side pot if there are still two or more active players betting.

See "Side Pot Procedures" on page 149 for more information on all-in bets.

Cash on the Table

If there is a sign saying "Cash plays," then cash in all denominations which a player puts on the table is part of that player's table stake in any game. A player may take cash from his pocket and put it on the table to add it to his stake at any time *between hands.*

Many cardrooms do not allow cash on the table. As soon as a player takes cash from his pocket, the dealer will immediately change it up for chips or call a chiprunner. If this occurs during the play of a hand, the dealer should change the money immediately, but say "That will play next hand." In some rooms, cash plays only if it is $100 bills.

In some jurisdictions, cash is not allowed on the table in any game. In such a case, a player must buy chips before beginning to play or at any time between hands that he wishes to increase his table stake. Players' checks are typically purchased from the dealer, from a chiprunner, from a floorperson, or at the casino cage.

The Basics of Poker

The basic rules of poker are simple. The objective of the game is to win the pot — that is, the money or chips placed in the center of the table. This is accomplished in one of two ways. A player can either show his opponents the best hand — which may be a high hand or a low hand, depending on the particular variation of poker being played — or he can bluff and convince them that he has the best hand. In some forms of poker, the best high hand and the best low hand each win half the pot. This variation is known as high-low split.

Each poker hand starts by seeding the pot with a token amount of money in the form of an ante, one or more blind bets, a forced "bring-in" bet, or a combination of these. If an ante is used, everyone must place a small percentage of the initial bet into the pot. If blinds are used, one or more players will be designated to post a bet or a partial bet before receiving any cards. Blinds usually are rotated around the table, so everyone pays their fair share.

During the play of a hand, opportunities to bet and raise occur after each round of cards is dealt. If at any time a player chooses not to continue in the hand, he may discard it in turn, thus forfeiting his interest in the pot. This means, of course, that he does not have to put any additional money into the pot.

If he is the bettor or raiser and no one calls his last bet, he wins the pot. If one or more players do call, then the person showing the best hand wins the pot.

Poker is as simple as that. Yet this basic set of rules, plus a few additional ones specific to each form of poker, produce a most wonderful game. A game that many people will play for a lifetime — some very seriously, but countless others for enjoyment alone. And a game that can provide you with a rewarding career as a poker dealer if you take your job seriously and learn your job well.

Rank of Cards

The ace is generally the highest card, followed by the king, queen, jack, ten, nine, eight, seven, six, five, four, trey, and deuce.

A card rank of "2" is called a deuce (there are no "twos" in a poker deck). A card rank of "3" is referred to as a trey.

The ace may be used as a low card for a low hand (as in lowball or any high-low split game) or to make a five-high straight 5-4-3-2-A (often called a "wheel" or "bicycle"). Exceptions occur in some forms of lowball such as "deuce-to-seven" lowball, where the ace is always high, and 7-5-4-3-2 (sometimes called a "wheel" in this game) is the best possible hand. These exception games are hardly ever spread in public cardrooms even though deuce-to-seven is sometimes the big money game during a major tournament. But even when this is the case it will only be played by a small number of people.

The Ranking of Hands

Seven-card stud and Texas hold 'em are the most common variations of poker played for high, where the highest ranking hand wins. These two games and most other forms of poker are played with a standard fifty-two-card deck. No joker is included. A deck consists of four different suits (all suits being equal) — spades, hearts, diamonds, and clubs — and each suit contains thirteen cards.

Although most forms of poker spread in public cardrooms are played with seven cards, the goal is to make the best five-card poker hand at the showdown. The ranking order for hands in high poker, based on their probability of occurrence — from least likely to most likely — is as follows:

Straight flush. Five cards of the same suit in sequence. An ace-high straight flush is referred to as a "royal flush" and is the best possible hand in poker played for high.[6]

---

[6]In high draw games using a joker, which can count as the fifth ace, five aces is the best hand.

Four of a kind. Four cards of the same rank, plus an unrelated fifth card that has no bearing on the hand's value.[7] The higher the rank of the four of a kind, the better the hand is.

Full house. Three cards of one rank and two cards of another rank. The rank of a full house is determined by the three of a kind, not by the pair except in hold 'em or Omaha where two or more players can have the same three of a kind.

Flush. Any five cards of the same suit. The cards are not in sequence, and the suit has no bearing on the rank of the flush. If more than one player holds a flush, the highest flush is determined by the rank of the individual cards, starting with the highest card.

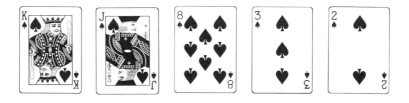

---

[7]An exception occurs in hold 'em when the four of a kind is on board. Now it is in everyone's hand and the person(s) with the highest card will win (or split) the pot. Note: The highest card could be the remaining board card.

Straight. Five cards in sequence, not all of the same suit.

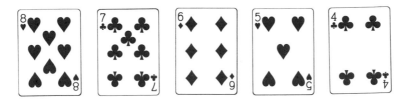

Three of a kind. Three cards of the same rank, plus two unrelated cards.

Two pair. Two cards of one rank, two cards of another rank, and one unrelated card. If two players each have two pair and their high pair is of the same rank, the winning hand is determined by the rank of the lower pair. If both lower pair are also of the same rank, then the winning hand is determined by the rank of the unrelated card.

One pair. Two cards of one rank, plus three unrelated cards. If two players hold the same rank of one pair, the rank of their side cards determines the best hand.

No pair. Five unrelated cards.

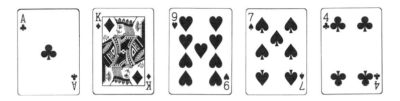

As a reminder, in the event that two or more hands tie in a particular category, the winning hand is determined by the rank of the unrelated cards, but no more than five cards are ever considered. Also, all suits are of equal value for determining hand rankings at the showdown.

The hand rankings listed are for high poker only. But in some forms of poker, the best low hand wins the pot, and in other forms — known as split-pot games — the best low hand, with certain qualifications, wins half the pot. As already mentioned, in most forms of low poker or split poker the best low hand is five-four-trey-deuce-ace, which is known as a wheel or a bicycle, and straights and flushes are disregarded for low.

In addition, we want to mention that "ace-to-five" lowball draw, which is still played in many cardrooms — particularly those in California — is played with a standard fifty-two-card deck, plus a joker, which counts as the lowest card not already in a player's hand.[8]

---

[8]Years ago only forms of draw poker were legal in California. This changed in 1987 when a Los Angeles court ruled that hold 'em and stud could also be spread. High draw quickly died

Betting Structures and Limits

There are four basic types of betting structures — structured (sometimes referred to as fixed) limit, spread limit, pot limit, and no limit. Most low-limit stud games are spread limit, while many other games, and most middle- or high-limit games are structured limit. These structures and certain variations are discussed on the following pages.

Structured limit means that if a player wants to bet or raise, it must be the exact amount specified by the structure (unless the player is going all-in). For example, limits specified as "$3 and $6" means that each bet and raise must be exactly $3 during early betting rounds and $6 during the latter betting rounds. The change over is always predetermined at some point about halfway through the hand.

Fourth street rule: An exception occurs in seven-card stud when the "fourth street rule" is in use.[9] In structured-limit stud the higher limit usually takes effect on fifth street. The fourth street rule allows any player to bet or raise either the lower or the higher limit on fourth street if an open pair shows in any player's hand. A high-limit raise after a low-limit bet is also allowed, but not vice versa.

Spread limit such as "$1 to $5" means that a player may bet any amount within that range ($1, $2, $3, $4, or $5) at any time on any betting round. Note the use of the word "and" for structured limits and "to" for spread limits.

---

out, but ace-to-five lowball has its adherents till this day.

[9]Almost all structured-limit stud games today use the fourth street rule.

In all cases, any raise must be at least equal to the bet or last raise in the current betting round. For example, suppose the limits are $1 to $4, and there is a $2 bet. The next player may simply call or fold, but to raise that player must make it $4, $5, or $6; a raise of $1 is not allowed since that is less than the bet. If the raise is $3 (making it $5 total), then any subsequent raise on that round of betting must be at least $3. This prevents the home game tactic of limiting one's exposure by making a minimum raise, thus eating up one of the allowed raises at minimal cost.

Even though there was a large bet or raise during one round of a spread-limit game, the minimum starting bet on the next round goes back to the lowest limit for that round of betting.

Mixed limit, such as $1-$3-$6, are commonly seen in Texas hold 'em. This means that it's a spread-limit game with betting limits of $1 to $3 at any time except that on the last betting round (river card) the limits go to $1 to $6. "$1-$4-$8-$8" (read as "one-four-double-eight") means that you can bet $1 to $4 during the first two rounds and $1 to $8 on the last two rounds.[10]

You might also see mixed limits in seven-card stud. The limits might allow a low spread through fourth street, then a higher spread on the last three rounds. If the fourth street rule is in use then the higher spread is allowed if an open pair shows on fourth street.[11]

Limit abbreviations are often used, especially in cardroom surveys. First, note above the use of the word "and" in structured limit and "to" in spread limit. To save space, or perhaps just to make it more readable, "$2 and $4" is often abbreviated "$2-$4."

---

[10]Many $1-$4-$8-$8 games use a $2 blind on the opening round. Thus, the smallest bet you can make in the first round is $2, not $1 as the name implies.

[11]At the time of this writing we know of only one cardroom that spreads a mixed-limit seven-card stud game.

Pot limit and **No limit** are beyond the scope of this handbook, but they are described in the glossary.

Note: Most cardrooms have a three-raise limit. That is, after an initial bet or blinds there may be no more than three raises. Some casinos allow four or even five raises. There should be a sign on the wall or on the podium indicating this policy.[12]

---

[12]As already stated, it is our opinion that a bet and four raises is the better policy. When only three raises are allowed many players are quick to take the action to the fourth level because they do not fear a reraise. Thus this rule, which is usually instituted by cardrooms in an attempt to keep their games from getting "too big" often has the opposite effect.

Part
3
Games Played

Games Played

Introduction

Most cardrooms spread only two or three kinds of poker —
and often only one set of limits for each game — although the
larger rooms may offer several limits and will spread any legal
game at any desired limit if enough players ask for it.

The game, betting limits, and structure will be posted on a
placard on or above the table. Usually only one game is played at
any given table. An exception is what are known as dual games
such as ½ hold 'em, ½ seven-card stud; or ½ hold 'em, ½ Omaha
eight-or-better. These games usually change with the dealer.

Other exceptions are the combination games such as HOSE
(hold 'em, Omaha eight-or-better, stud, and stud eight-or-better),
or HORSE (which is HOSE plus razz). In these games the type of
poker changes after a designated amount of hands — usually eight
or ten. Combination games are usually dealt in alphabetical order
after the player who draws the high card selects the initial game.

The most commonly spread games in public cardrooms are
seven-card stud, Texas hold 'em, and to a smaller extent Omaha
and Omaha eight-or-better. These games are described briefly
below, with more details on the following pages. Variations such
as seven-card stud eight-or-better (high-low split), high draw
jacks-or-better to open, lowball (draw poker where the lowest
hand wins), razz (seven-card stud lowball), seven-card stud
deuce-to-seven lowball, pineapple, crazy pineapple, Chinese
poker, pai gow poker, Let It Ride™, Caribbean Stud,™ and others
are spread in some rooms.

Quick Overview of Games

Seven-Card Stud

Seven-card stud is the same game you have probably played at home on the kitchen table, and for that reason it is frequently the low-limit game of choice for a tourist in public casinos. Seven-card stud is almost universal, with most rooms offering it in $1-$3, $1-$4 or $1-$5 spread limits. Usually the player with the lowest door card (first up card, a.k.a. third street) must "bring in" the action with a minimum bet of $1 (50¢ in some $1-$3 games), although the player may open for any amount up to the table limit. After the first betting round, the action begins with the highest hand showing and proceeds with the high hand acting first until the winner is determined at the showdown.

Texas Hold 'em

Texas hold 'em is very popular among today's players, and it is the game played in the final event in many major tournaments. Position is very important in hold 'em, giving the dealer an advantage by being last to act on each betting round (except the first round when the big blind is last to act). Since the house dealer is actually distributing the cards, a dealer "button" determines where the action starts. The cards are dealt and all action takes place just as if the player having the button were dealing the hand. At least one blind bet, and usually two blind bets, must be posted by the first player(s) clockwise from the button before any cards are dealt, and each player receives two cards face down (their "hole cards"). Eventually there will be five community cards in the center of the table. At the showdown, each player uses any five out of the seven cards available to him (his two hole cards and the five community cards) to make the best possible poker hand.

Omaha

Omaha, a variation on Texas hold 'em, is often played high-low-split with an eight-or-better required for low, but it is also occasionally spread as high only. The game structure and community cards are the same as in hold 'em except that each player receives four cards instead of two. At the showdown, exactly two hole cards and three board cards must be used to make a five-card hand. Any such combination may be used for high, and the same or any other such combination of two hole cards and three board cards may be used for a low hand. (Note: A particular card or cards may be used as part of the high combination as well as the low combination. For example if a player is holding

and the board is

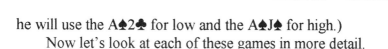

he will use the A♠2♣ for low and the A♠J♠ for high.)

Now let's look at each of these games in more detail.

Seven-Card Stud

The deal always starts in seat one. (See the chapter entitled "Table Layout" on page 63 in Part Four of this book.) Each player receives a total of seven cards, beginning with two down and one up. After the first betting round, each player receives another up card, and there is another round of betting. This repeats until each player has four up cards. The seventh card is dealt face down, and there is a final round of betting, making five rounds of betting in all. After all the action is complete, there is a showdown to determine the winner.

Typical procedures and house rules for seven-card stud:

1. In most games, an ante is posted by each player before the cards are dealt, but there is no ante in the small spread-limit games offered by most cardrooms in Nevada.

2. Each player is dealt a starting hand of two down cards (hole cards) and one card face up (called the "door card"). If a player's first or second hole card is accidentally turned up, the third card is dealt face down. If two cards are dealt face up, the player's hand is declared dead, and any ante or forced bet is returned to the player.

3. The lowest door card must start the action with a forced "bring-in" bet, typically 50¢ in a $1-$3 game or $1 in a $1-$4 or $1-$5 game, but the player may choose to make any bet within the limits of the game. If two or more players have the same low card showing, the bring-in is determined by suit in alphabetical order (clubs, diamonds, hearts, spades) with clubs being first. (In poker, this is the only case where the suits are treated differently.)

4. On subsequent rounds of betting, the highest hand showing is first to act, but it is not a forced bet. If two hands are equal (disregarding suit) then the first such hand clockwise from the dealer acts first.

41

5. If the player holding the highest hand is all-in then the first player clockwise from that position is first to act. (This is as if the all-in player had money but had checked.)

6. If a player after making a forced entry bet folds his hand before the burn, the seat will not receive any more cards. If however, the dealer has burned (or it is a tie) the seat will take an additional card. (This rule may vary between cardrooms.)

7. If the dealer deals a down card to an empty seat (first or second card) and the error cannot be corrected, it is a misdeal. If it occurs on an up card, it will be corrected by moving the cards to the proper position. If it occurs on the final down card and cannot be corrected, the cards will play as dealt. (Floorperson's decision.)

8. If a dealer burns and deals a card before a round of betting has been completed, that card will not play. The floorperson must be called to make a decision on how to continue.

9. If a dealer burns two cards or fails to burn a card, the cards will be moved to the correct position to rectify the error if possible. If it happens on the river card and there is no way to tell which card was received, the cards will play as dealt — call a floorperson.

10. If the dealer turns any player's last card face up, a floorperson must be called for a decision. If the player who received his or her card "up" is the first person dealt, all the other players will receive their cards "up" and the action will proceed as normal with the person who was high on sixth street being first to act. If any other player receives his or her last card "up" then there is no action.[13]

11. If the "fourth street rule" is in effect (structured-limit and mixed-limit games only) and any player makes an open pair on the fourth card, then any player has the option of betting

---

[13] In some cardrooms the player whose down card was exposed has the option of declaring himself all-in, and the other players continue in a side pot.

or raising either the low limit or the high limit. (This is sometimes referred to as making either a "single" or "double" size bet.) However, once any player chooses to use the higher limit another player cannot raise the lower amount.

12. A player who calls when he is beaten by his opponent's up cards is not entitled to a refund. (House rules may vary on this. In some low-limit games catering to tourists, a player who calls when beaten by a betting opponent's up cards may be given a refund from the pot one time as a courtesy. Only the last call will be refunded. There will be no refund if the player bet or raised on the last round.)

13. A player must have exactly seven cards shown face up in order to win. Any other number of cards may constitute a dead hand. (Also, all seven cards must be different. For example, you cannot win a pot with two aces of spades in your hand. This is a floorperson's decision.)

14. If a player turns down any of his up cards after a bet has been made, or if he pushes his hand toward the dealer without turning all seven cards face up, his hand is considered folded, and he concedes all rights to the pot. Remember, as a dealer, kill that hand once it has been released towards you.

15. If a player picks up his up cards and mixes them with his hole cards to examine them, the hand is still live provided the bet has been called. However, if the player then lays the cards face down on the table the hand is considered folded. Furthermore, picking up "up cards" when there has been no call is cause to declare that player's hand dead if it causes anyone to act after him. Even heads-up.

16. To avoid running out of cards, seven-card stud games are usually limited to a maximum of seven or eight players. In spite of this, there are occasionally too few cards left in the deck to give each remaining player a seventh card. The floorperson must be called and will usually instruct the dealer to put up a single community card. The community card will be placed face up in the center of the table and will act as the seventh card in each player's hand. The player who had the

highest hand showing on sixth street is still first to act. If the dealer has dealt a down card to one or more players before he realizes he doesn't have enough cards then the floorperson will usually instruct the dealer to "shuffle the burns" and then the remaining players will receive a seventh card as usual.[14]

17. If the dealer begins to deal the next round of up cards before the action is complete, then those cards dealt will be taken back and the action completed. Enough cards will then be added to the misdealt cards (face down) so that the number of cards taken out of action is equal to the number of players remaining in the pot. The dealer then burns and deals the next round, and the game proceeds normally. (This is a floorperson's decision.)

---

[14]In some rooms shuffling the burns is the first choice.

Seven-Card Stud
High-Low-Split

This is the same as seven-card stud described on the preceding pages except at the showdown the pot is split between the best high hand and the best low hand. An eight or better is usually required to qualify for low. If no one qualifies for low then the high hand takes the entire pot. This game is also called stud eight-or-better.

Split games use the lower betting limit on third and fourth street and the upper betting limit on subsequent streets, with an open pair not affecting the limit. Specifically, if someone pairs their door card on fourth street only a "single" size bet can be made. In addition, aces may be used for either high or low, and straights and flushes do not impair the value of a hand for low.

Cards speak. There is no declaration for high or low. A player may use any five cards to make his best high hand and either the same or any other grouping of five cards to make his best low hand, thus making it possible for one player to win the entire pot. In some cases, a low straight or flush may win both high and low.

Razz (Seven-Card Stud Low)

The lowest hand wins the pot. Aces are low, and straights and flushes do not impair the low card value of a hand, so the best possible hand is 5-4-3-2-A (often called a "wheel" or "bicycle").

The format is similar to standard seven-card stud, except that the high card (king is high) is required to make the bring-in bet on the first round,[15] and the lowest hand showing acts first on all subsequent rounds. Aces are always low in razz.

1. The best hand is 5-4-3-2-A.
2. Straights and flushes are not detrimental to the value of a hand.
3. High card by suit starts the action with a mandatory bring-in (king is high), then on subsequent rounds the lowest hand showing bets first.
4. In structured-limit games, the lower limit applies on third and fourth street, and the higher limit applies hereafter. The fourth street rule is not applicable to this game.

All other seven-card stud rules apply unless otherwise noted.

---

[15]In the case of a tie, such as two players having a queen showing and no king is showing, the bring-in is determined by suit in the opposite order as for standard seven-card stud. That is, spades are first, followed by hearts, diamonds, and clubs.

Seven-Card Stud
Deuce-to-Seven Low

The lowest hand wins the pot. Aces are high, and straights and flushes *do* impair the value of a hand, so the best possible hand is 7-5-4-3-2, but not all the same suit. (In this game, this hand may sometimes be called a "wheel" or "bicycle."").

The format is similar to standard seven-card stud, except the high card by suit (ace is high) is required to make the bring-in bet on the first round, and the lowest hand showing acts first on all subsequent rounds.

1. The best hand is 7-5-4-3-2 (not all the same suit).
2. Straights and flushes count as high hands.
3. High card starts the action with a mandatory bring-in (ace is high), then on subsequent rounds the lowest hand showing bets first.
4. In fixed-limit games, the lower limit applies on third and fourth street, and the higher limit applies thereafter. The fourth street rule is not applicable to this game.

All other seven-card stud rules apply unless otherwise noted. (Note: This game is very rare and at the time of this writing we do not know of any cardroom that offers it, but it is sometimes played as a high-limit side game during the major tournaments.)

47

Five-Card Stud

This is the original version of stud poker. Each player gets one down card and one up card to start, and there is a round of betting. Each player then gets one more up card, and another round of betting. This repeats until each player has four up cards (a total of five cards with four rounds of betting).

Five card stud is seldom played any more, probably because there is generally very little action. Often the first bet wins the antes, and the hand is over.

Some cardrooms may spread a version of five-card stud using a short deck. All the deuces through sixes are removed, leaving a thirty-two-card deck. This causes pairs and better hands to occur more frequently, making it a more interesting game. Also, it reverses the frequency, and hence the values, of the flush and full house. You are not likely to encounter this game in Nevada except possibly during tournaments, but it is spread in some of the larger cardrooms in California.

Texas Hold 'em

In Texas hold 'em, each player receives two down cards as their initial hand, and there is a round of betting. Three board cards called "the flop" are then turned simultaneously by the dealer, and another round of betting occurs. The next two board cards, known as fourth street and fifth street or the "turn" and the "river," are turned one at a time with a round of betting after each one.

The board cards are community cards, and each player uses any five of the seven available cards (both hole cards and three from the board, one in their hand and four on the board, or the five board cards) to make the best possible hand. A player using all of the board cards to make his best hand is said to be "playing the board."

Typical Procedures and House Rules for Texas Hold 'em

Texas hold 'em has become the most popular form of poker in the cardrooms of the south and west and is growing rapidly as the game of choice in most other locations. Even though there are many different variations of hold 'em, most rules and procedures have become "standard" in many cardrooms. They are described below.

1. Position is very important in all poker games, but especially so in hold 'em. Being last to act is advantageous. To give each player an equal number of hands in each position, hold 'em incorporates a disk called a "dealer button," which indicates the player who in principle is the dealer for the current hand. This button moves from player to player just as the deal passes around the table in a home game. The button (player with the dealer button) is last to receive cards on the initial deal and has the right of last action on all betting rounds except the first (where the blinds have last action).

49

2. Instead of an ante, one or more blind bets are used to stimulate action and initiate play. Blinds are posted before the players receive any cards. The blinds are "live." That is, each blind counts as part of that player's bet. The last blind is known as the "big blind." (In some cases the structure for a specific game or situation requires part or all of a particular blind to be "dead." Dead money is not part of a player's bet and is taken into the center of the pot before the action begins.)

3. In most games, blinds are posted by players in the first one, two, or three positions clockwise from the button. Action is initiated on the first betting round by the first player after the last blind, who has not yet entered the pot. Action proceeds clockwise and the big blind is last to act with the option to raise or to check if there has been no previous raise. On all subsequent betting rounds, the action is begun by the first active player clockwise from the button, and the person having the dealer button is last to act.

4. If a player's hole card is exposed due to a dealer error, he may not keep the exposed card. After completing the deal, the dealer will exchange the exposed card with the top card on the deck and place the exposed card on top of the deck, usually face up. The exposed card will be used as the burn card after all the action before the flop is completed. (Some cardrooms vary in this.) If two or more cards are exposed on the deal, it is a misdeal.

5. If the flop has too many cards, or if the flop is put up before all the betting is completed, it usually will be taken back and reshuffled, except the burn card, which will remain burned. No new burn card will be used.[16]

---

[16]Procedures 5 through 7, as well as declaring a hand dead as in number 8, generally require a floorperson's decision. Since a floorperson's decision is final, and not all think alike, these procedures may vary from time to time

6. If the dealer turns up the fourth board card (the "turn" card) before the betting is complete, the card will not play. After completion of the betting, the next card is burned and the card that would have been the fifth card is put up in the fourth card's place. After betting is completed, the dealer will reshuffle the deck, including the card that was taken out of play and turn the fifth card. There is no new burn.

7. If the fifth card (the "river" card) is turned up before betting is complete, it is reshuffled in the same manner as in rule 6 above.

8. The winning hand must show both cards face up on the table; one card up and the other face down is not a valid hand. Both hole cards must be shown even if playing the board. Too many or too few cards constitutes a fouled hand which may be declared dead.

9. A new player or a player who has missed one or more blinds may not receive a hand between the button and the blinds or on the button. He must wait until the button passes. (Some rooms allow receiving a hand in these positions by posting a big blind.)

10. When starting a new game, the players generally draw for the button. However, in some cardrooms it starts at the last seat so that seat number one has the first blind.

11. If a player leaves the table for any reason and the blinds pass his position, the dealer will put a missed blind button at the player's position. When the player returns he may resume play immediately (but generally not before the button has passed his seat) by posting the total amount of blinds for the game, or he may wait for the big blind. If he chooses to make up the blinds, the small blind is "dead" money and goes to the center of the pot while the big blind is live. In games with only one blind there will be no dead money. This varies in some cardrooms. See "Button and Blinds Rules on page 90" for more details.

12. If a player pays both of the blinds as they come to him but then leaves the table, the button moves to his position anyway, and a "dead button" will be announced. Many cardrooms (mainly

outside Nevada) use an "advancing button rule" that eliminates the dead button. See "Button and Blinds Rules" on page 90 for more details.

Omaha

Omaha is a variation on Texas hold 'em, and it is identical in structure with two exceptions:
1. Each player initially receives four hole cards.
2. At showdown, exactly two of a player's hole cards and three of the community cards must be used to make up a five-card hand.

Omaha is often played as a high-low-split game with an eight or better required to qualify for low. Each player makes up a five-card high hand using any two hole cards along with any three community cards, and he also makes up a five-card low hand using any two hole cards along with any three community cards. These two hands may be made up using the same or any other combination of two hole cards and three board cards.

Note: It is impossible for any player to make a low hand unless there are at least three *different rank* cards that are eight or lower (including aces) on the board. If no one qualifies for low then the high hand wins the entire pot.

Omaha is probably the most difficult poker game to deal because the larger possible number of five-card hand combinations make the board more difficult to read. Because of the high-low-split there are often five or more players still active at the showdown. At the end of the action, several players may turn their hands up simultaneously and expect the dealer to read them instantly without error.

It's not possible to read several hands instantly, but there are some techniques to aid you in reading Omaha hands. In a nutshell, the main "trick" is to examine the board before trying to read hands so that you know what to expect. Be specific in your mind about what you're looking for. Don't worry about monster hands. If someone has four of a kind or a straight flush, they won't let you overlook it. Here are some examples:

- If there is a pair on the board, you are not simply looking for a full house; you're looking for a card of the same rank as the pair, and if you find one then look for something else to go with the board. Also look for a pair in a player's hand that matches any card on the board.

- If there are three suited cards on the board, you are not simply looking for a flush; you are looking for two cards of that specific suit.

- If a jack, queen, and nine are on board, you are not simply looking for a straight; you are looking for a ten. If you find a ten then look for either a king or an eight in that hand.

- If a low is possible (i.e., there are at least three cards on board of rank eight or lower) then you are looking for the two lowest cards that are not on the board. If there are four "wheel cards" on board then you are looking for the missing rank and any other wheel card.

Part
4
Dealer Information

Dealer Information

Introduction

We now come to the main section of *The Professional Poker Dealer's Handbook* — the part of the book where we discuss proper dealing technique. Or, put another way, this is where you learn how to deal.

Even though all the topics in this section are important, we recommend that you pay special attention to "Characteristics of a Professional Dealer," "Mechanical Skills," "Pitching Down Cards," "Getting a Fill," "Controlling Bets and Raises," and "Reading Players' Hands." In our experience, these are the areas that are generally the most troublesome at the poker tables and the most upsetting to players.

To have a successful career as a poker dealer you need to be extremely focused on the game. This can only be done once you have mastered all the topics in this section. When that is accomplished you should find your job to be enjoyable as well as rewarding.

Differences between Poker and Pit Games

Why might a prospective dealer choose to learn poker rather than the pit games such as blackjack, craps, roulette, etc.? There are many reasons. Here are just a few of them:

1. You sit down while you work. This could be a significant benefit for someone with back, leg, or hip problems.
2. Most dealers keep their own tokes. Occasionally this results in inequities because you may push several large pots to someone who tokes well, and at other times the generous tippers may not be at your table. However, for the most part your income will be directly related to how well you treat your customers, and how accurately and efficiently you run your game — thus giving you an incentive to improve your skills.
3. You will get to know many regular customers who play the same game day after day. This is rare in the pit games.
4. You have a fixed amount of money in the dealer's bank. Although you may be responsible if the bank is short when the next dealer pushes you, you don't have to sign for fills and put up with other checks and balances.
5. In most cardrooms you are allowed, even encouraged to play poker in your own room, often while still "on the clock." (That is, being paid for your time.) This is a benefit: Even if you don't want to play poker, other dealers will play — and dealers are good tokers. Most casinos prohibit pit dealers from playing any "in house" games except for poker or slots (not progressives) and never "on the clock."

It is rarely a requirement that you play poker, but cardroom managers generally like dealers who play. For the management, it's like having a free proposition player to help start and maintain games. Sure, you are being paid your regular hourly rate for your time, but you are allowed to play only because there are too many dealers for the number of games currently in progress, so you would be paid anyway.

But it's not only the management who benefits from dealers who like to play. Remember: If there is no game, you do not get to deal. Helping to start or maintain a game helps the cardroom, the dealers, and the players.

A dealer's conduct while playing in a game is very important as it sets an example for other players. Courtesy and friendliness pay big dividends later when you are dealing. If playing while on break, it is in poor taste to use tokes directly from your pocket to enter the game. You are using money that your customers just gave you to try to beat them. To avoid this, convert your tokes to chips or cash before entering the game.

What's Important?

What are the most important attributes of a good dealer?
1. Accuracy
2. Technique
3. Focus
4. Efficiency
5. Restraint

Yes, speed is important, but never at the expense of accuracy or technique. Speed develops through experience, provided accuracy and technique are maintained and improved.

Many dealers attempt to get more hands out by rushing. This not only makes them more prone to errors, but the sacrifice of good technique limits their eventual speed. If you concentrate on technique and efficiency, your speed will gradually increase naturally, and you will soon be faster than the dealer who rushes.

We also want to address the importance of restraint. Poker plays best when it is fast paced and error-free. This requires a dealer who is completely focused on the game and who takes part in no extraneous talking. (An exception to this might occur in the smallest seven-card stud games where most of the players appear to be more interested in socializing rather than playing poker.)

Each casino sets forth specific rules or policies to govern a dealer's appearance and reliability. You can probably keep your job by just adhering to the letter of the law, or you can contribute to the spirit of the situation, which will yield much greater benefits. What is sincerely hoped is that each dealer will see, sense, and feel his or her level of proficiency as a professional. If you continue to raise your individual expectations of yourself, you will most likely improve your skills (and income) with very little additional effort. Remember that everything you do to please your customers and your superiors is also likely to result in more and bigger tokes. *A pleasant and positive attitude returns values many times the effort involved.*

Here is a fundamental truth: An instructor can offer knowledge of the game, mechanical skills, and technique, but he cannot instill it. In other words, this and everything in this book will be just words with no real meaning unless you, the individual, take the initiative and accept the responsibility of understanding and learning.

One of the most difficult situations that can occur in a cardroom, is when there is a dispute at the table and the dealer cannot accurately explain to the floorperson exactly what happened because he was talking and not giving his job the full attention it deserves. To repeat: Always make sure that you use restraint and are always focused on the game.

Characteristics of a Professional Dealer

Let's look more closely at the attributes that go together to make a true "professional" dealer:

Characteristic No 1: Accuracy. Getting the right cards to the right players at the right time smoothly and without exposing cards, turning board cards at the right time, keeping the bets and side pots straight, making change correctly, getting the correct rake unobtrusively, reading hands correctly, pushing the pot to the player with the best hand, splitting pots correctly when necessary, and so forth.

Characteristic No. 2: Mechanical skills. Technique! The ability to shuffle and deal without exposing cards, handle chips, and the like.

Characteristic No. 3: Knowledge of the games. Knowing and understanding the rules of each game, how the game is dealt, and the house policies and procedures.

Characteristic No. 4: Ability to control the game. Being able to maintain the game pace. That is, the ability to keep the game moving, prevent out-of-turn actions, avoid unnecessary delays, without rushing either yourself or the players. Remember, always use an open hand — never point — at a player when it is their turn to act. (You may point with your eyes, but *never stare* at a player who may be taking a little extra time.)

Characteristic No. 5: Positive attitude. A manner of conveying professionalism that makes the experience of playing poker enjoyable and rewarding.

Characteristic No. 6: Professional demeanor. Proper posture and attitude communicate professionalism as does courtesy and kindness.

Characteristic No. 7: Ability to deal with customers. Besides attitude and personality, this includes diplomacy, etiquette, and knowing when to call for the floorperson.

Characteristic No. 8: Appearance. One's dress, grooming, and personal hygiene are essential to a professional demeanor.

Characteristic No. 9: Reliability. The ability to do your job properly and to be available and prepared when needed.

Characteristic No. 10: Restraint. The ability to be quiet, keep your full attention focused on the game, and to decline to partake in any extraneous conversations not directly related to the hand in progress.

These attributes of a professional dealer are distinctly different, yet they overlap and complement each other. The thrust of the material contained herein is directed toward those attributes that an instructor can develop and enhance — primarily knowledge of the games, mechanical skills, accuracy, and restraint.

Table Layout

Unlike the square, round, or octagonal tables often used for home poker, a casino poker table is stretched out to a long rectangle with round ends. The surface of the table is padded and covered with felt or nylon fabric, and a padded rail surrounds the table except at the dealer's position. Depending on the particular game being played, the table will be set up for anywhere from seven to twelve players, plus the dealer who sits at the center of one of the long sides.[17]

The players' seats are numbered, starting with the "one" seat at the dealer's immediate left and continuing clockwise. Like the seat numbers (which are seldom printed on the table), all action proceeds clockwise around the table, skipping from the seat on the dealer's right to seat one. The action begins at a starting point determined according to the specific game rules.

The dealer's position at the table is called "the box." In front of the dealer is a rack, or "bank" (see next section). Each dealer's turn at a particular table (usually twenty or thirty minutes) is called a "down."

Somewhere on the table, typically just to the dealer's left, there will be a placard showing the name of the game being played, the betting limits, and the rake. Sometimes this information will be on a sign hanging over the table. Occasionally a cardroom manager will change a game's structure or rake without notifying all of the dealers, so it is important for a dealer to check the placard each time before sitting down.

Just to the right of the rack is a drop slot with the table number. Usually it has a place where the raked chips are placed and a handle at the back that drops the rake without the need for the dealer to touch the chips again. On some older tables, however, there is just

---

[17]Games with more than eight players for stud and ten players for hold 'em are very rare.

63

a small circle painted on the table where the raked chips are placed until the hand is over and a slot where they are dropped. In either case, the rake drops into a locked box under the table that is changed by security once per shift.

In some cases there may be a separate box or slot for a jackpot rake, usually on the dealer's left.

In most cardrooms the dealer puts any tokes in his or her shirt pocket, but in some casinos there is a separate box for tokes (possibly because of a uniform with no pockets).[18] Also, in some jurisdictions each dealer owns his or her bank (see next section); in such a case, tokes are usually just put in the dealer's bank.[19]

---

[18]In Atlantic City, and in some Indian casinos, where all dealers pool tokes, a separate box is used for that purpose. We disagree with this policy, as it hinders the incentive to be as productive.

[19]When a dealer carries his own bank he should be especially careful to make his moves clear when making change to avoid suspicion that he is shortchanging either the player or the pot.

The Dealer's Rack

The dealer's rack, or bank, sits in a cutout in the table immediately in front of the dealer. The rack provides chips needed to sell to the players and to make change as necessary during a hand. In some rooms the rack is picked up and stored somewhere when there is no game at that table. In other rooms where the rack is permanent, a locking cover is placed over the rack.

Unlike the pit games, the poker dealer's rack always contains a predetermined amount of money and chips. When the dealer sells chips to a player, the cash is placed in the rack rather than being dropped down a slot, so the total in the rack remains constant. It is the dealer's responsibility that the rack contains the correct amount when leaving the table. The next dealer counts the rack, and the outgoing dealer may be required to make up any shortages.

The incoming dealer can count most of the chips in the rack, over the outgoing dealer's shoulder while waiting to push into that game. He would then immediately count any cash in the well keeping the game going, and report any irregularities within five minutes.

Some rooms allow shortages up to a specified amount (e.g., $3) without requiring the dealer to make it up. Know what the policy is in your room, and report such a shortage to the next dealer when you are pushed. Similarly, an overage up to the same threshold may not need to be reported immediately.

Each cardroom has its own standard way of organizing the rack. Regardless of personal preference, each dealer should keep the rack as close as possible to that standard so that it can be easily counted by the next dealer. Likewise, any cash in the rack should be kept sorted. When cash comes in during a hand, the dealer should put it in the well, then put it in sorted order when the hand is over.[20]

To avoid requiring a fill immediately after starting a new game, the floorperson will usually bring a "game bank" (one or more racks of chips) to the table. You should count it and verify that it is the amount that the "fill slip" says it is since it becomes your responsibility to make sure that the monies stay correct. Sell the players' their initial chips from the game bank, and keep those chips and cash separate from your rack. The floorperson will pick up the game bank and the cash, and it must total the same amount that was given to you. The floorperson must count it before leaving the table.

In some jurisdictions the dealer's rack is owned by the dealer instead of by the house, and the dealer carries the rack from table to table. In this case it is each dealer's responsibility to bring enough money to work each day to buy chips to fill the rack. Such a rack is not necessarily a fixed amount, but management usually requires a specified minimum.

See also "Getting a Fill on page 88."

---

[20]When a hand is in progress and a player makes a bet with a large bill or chip requiring change the dealer should make change from the pot whenever possible. This will reduce the need for fills and help keep the game fast paced. However, in low-limit games leaving cash in the pot is not recommended. The theory is that having more chips on the table makes for more action and a longer lasting game.

Counting the Rack

In many cardrooms it is necessary to count the dealer's rack when you sit down at a table. This is to protect yourself in case the rack is short. The problem is that some dealers make this their top priority, allowing it to take precedence over the game. It is very annoying to the players to have to wait while each new dealer counts the rack.

Typically, you have five minutes in which to report a shortage, and you will not be held responsible if you report it within the allotted time. Therefore, the most important thing is to get the game going again. Here is the recommended way of pushing a dealer and counting the bank:

1. Approach the table preferably to the dealer's left, and tap him or her lightly on the shoulder. Typically you will have time to do the next two steps while waiting for the current hand to finish.

2. Read the game placard. The game or some of the parameters (limits, rake, etc.) may have been changed since the last time you dealt that table. Don't embarrass yourself by dealing the wrong game or taking the wrong rake.

3. Look over the dealer's shoulder and start counting the rack. Count the full stacks of chips and, if possible, the rolls of coins. By the time you sit down the job is already half finished.

4. Shuffle and deal the first hand. Whenever you have a moment during a lull in the action, count the partial stacks, and estimate the amount in loose coins. (If there is nearly a full roll of loose quarters, use a card as a measure. The width of a card is equal to eight dollars in quarters.)

5. By the time the first hand is over, you should know within a couple of dollars how much is in the rack in chips and coins. Take the cash from the well, and count it. This will take only a few seconds if the previous dealer kept the bills organized by denomination and you are ready to deal the next hand.

6.   If you do discover a shortage, call the floorperson over and report it. Meanwhile, begin dealing the next hand. Don't keep the players waiting.

7.   If the shortage hasn't been made up before you are pushed, tell the next dealer how much it is off and that it has been reported.

8.   Don't make up a shortage by shortchanging the pot. If you are caught, you could lose your job and/or your gaming card.

9.   If the rack is over a minimal amount tell the next dealer when you're pushed and inform the floorperson at the first opportunity.[21] (A large overage is probably due to an error on a fill.)

---

[21]If the rack is off by a small amount, wait until you leave the box before you inform the floorperson. On the other hand, if the rack is off by a larger amount you will need to call the floorperson immediately. The amounts will be defined by your cardroom.

Mechanical Skills

The basic mechanical techniques required of a casino poker dealer are described below and on the following pages. Unfortunately, many of these skills are almost impossible to learn without an instructor to demonstrate, no matter how detailed the written description. Nevertheless, you should read and re-read each description to learn the best technique.

Mechanical Skill No. 1: Spreading. To spread a deck, take the deck in your right hand (even if you're lefthanded) with the thumb and middle finger holding the narrow ends of the deck and your index finger on the side of the deck. Lay the deck face up on the table, and slide it from left to right making a semi-circle. While spreading the deck, the index finger applies only light pressure, and the thumb and middle finger only guide the deck at the ends. There's no need to break the deck exactly in half; that's five seconds wasted. Examine the deck starting from the right, going in groups of three-three-three-four; that is A-2-3, 4-5-6, 7-8-9, 10-J-Q-K, which is faster than counting up thirteen cards and you are more likely to spot a missing card.

Mechanical Skill No. 2. Scramble. Use your fingers and palms, moving the cards in a circular motion with your hands rotating and releasing the cards.[22] Mix the cards for approximately two to three seconds, making sure that all of the cards are involved. Do an especially good scramble whenever the deck is changed.

Mechanical Skill No. 3: Shuffle. When finished scrambling, gather the cards into a small pile, still face down, then pick them up on

---

[22]If you saw the movie "Karate Kid" you will know how to use the "wax on, wax off" motion, but do it simultaneously with both hands.

edge *facing away from yourself,* and square up the deck. Place the squared deck about two inches in front of the rack. The "riffle" shuffle is done in four steps with the top card of each half of the deck changing sides when you shuffle, as follows:

A. Hold the bottom half of the deck with the thumb and middle finger of your left hand. Grasp the top half of the deck with the thumb and middle finger of your right hand. Keeping a firm hold on the cards, take off the top half of the deck, set it on the table to the right of the lower half, and slide it to the left until the ends are together. Do this by feel, not by sight. There is no need to place them precisely or to have a "V" between the halves. Just put the ends flush together.

B. Place your hands over the cards, but keep them relaxed. The weight of your arms should be on the heels of your hands. Put the soft part of your thumbs against each half of the deck and your index fingers above the deck but not touching the cards. The rest of your fingers go behind the deck to keep it from sliding away, your finger tips should be on the table rather than gripping the deck. In one motion, tilt the deck up using your thumbs only, slide the halves of the deck inward, and continue the upward thumb motion to release the cards through the thumbs with no pressure on the cards. The shuffle should be nearly silent since you are not bending the cards. Think of it as *allowing* the cards to shuffle; you are only guiding them.

C. Push the halves of the deck together about half way, straightening the deck as you go. Release the deck before it starts to bind.

D. Place your thumb tips together at the back of the deck and your middle fingers at the ends of the deck at the front corners. Bring the two halves of the deck all the way together, lifting slightly so they will slide together more easily, then "pinch" the deck to square it. The "pinch" consists of bringing your middle fingers and thumbs together at the corner of the deck with pressure on the ends of the deck; this is the *only* way we square up the deck.

Mechanical Skill No. 4: Box. To box the cards (also called a "strip shuffle") hold the deck in your right hand, and anchor your left hand by placing your little finger on the table. Your right hand now brings the deck towards your left hand in a smooth, straight, horizontal "shuttle" motion close to the table. Using your left hand, grasp about ten cards off the top of the deck, and carry the deck out from under. Follow the small group of cards down to the table with your left index finger to prevent it from sliding around. Repeat four or five times, keeping the deck level, and place the last portion of the deck on top of the pile on the table. Square the deck with a pinch as described in step 3D above.

You then shuffle twice more, releasing the deck before each shuffle. Always try to make sure the top card changes sides when you shuffle.

Mechanical Skill No. 5: Release the deck. Always make an obvious release of the deck before cutting the cards. This is done automatically when gathering antes in stud games, but in flop games you must make *the obvious release.*

Mechanical Skill No. 6: Cut. Place the cut card about two inches in front of the deck, keeping your other hand clear of the deck as you do this. With a one-handed forward motion, cut the top half of the deck onto the cut card, place the remaining half of the deck on top of the first half, pick it up, and place it in your left hand as described in "Holding the Deck," keeping the deck level as you do so. (Note: Make sure that you never cover the top of the deck with your free hand or turn the deck over, known as rolling the deck.)

Mechanical Skill No. 7: Suiting. To suit a deck, separate the cards according to suit, then arrange each suit in numerical order, ace through king. Arrange the suits diamonds, clubs, hearts, and spades so that the ace of spades is showing on top. This is done to prepare the decks for use as a set-up or to check that the deck is correct when a jackpot occurs. (The process of suiting decks is usually done by a group of dealers and is commonly referred to as a "card party.")

Mechanical Skill No. 8: Setups. Players may ask for a "setup" when they want different cards in the game. A setup consists of two suited decks of cards. Call for a setup only when requested by a player and you don't have a suited deck in the well.[23] Do not call for a setup if a player only asks for a deck change; simply change to the other deck from the well. Scramble face up, then face down. (Always scramble any deck coming out of the well.) Of course if that deck is suited you will spread it as described above. When putting a used deck in the well, be sure that the top card showing is not the ace of spades. (Don't cause the next dealer to be embarrassed by spreading a used deck that he thought was suited.)

Don't hold up the game waiting for a setup. If it has not arrived by the time you're ready to shuffle for the next hand, apologize to the players and tell them you'll get the setup next hand.

When the setup arrives, take the deck you've been using and the deck from the well, place them crossed, face to face, and hand them over your shoulder to the person bringing the setup. The two new decks will be placed on the table in front of you face down. Verify that they are different color backs, and place the deck in the well that was the same color deck just taken out of play. (Always change color when a new setup is brought into play.) Spread the new deck face up (see above) then turn it face down and make sure the backs are all the same color as you scramble.

Mechanical Skill No. 9: Cutting chips. Cradle a stack of twenty chips in three fingers, holding it with your thumb and leaving your index finger free. Holding it at reading distance, use your index finger to lift up the sixth check, to roll all but the first five chips around your thumb, or to roll the bottom five forward with your

---

[23]In some high limit games the deck is changed every thirty minutes and a new setup is brought in on the hour, thus eliminating requests.

thumb. With practice you should not have to watch what you're doing from here on.

Set that first stack of five chips on the table where you want to count off the stack. Set the remainder of the stack down at least one inch away, and slide it up against the stack of five with your thumb and little finger. Slide your index finger across the stack of five, taking your third and forth fingers away temporarily as you do so, and hinge up the bigger stack against your thumb and little finger, leaving another stack of five against the first. Slide back on the tip of your little finger, set the remainder of the stack down, slide it against the second stack, and repeat the hinging action. Be sure to slide your index finger across the last two stacks to check that the last stack matches the others.

Mechanical Skill No. 10: Making change. When making change for a bet, first announce the amount being taken out of the piece (e.g., "three out of twenty"), and drop that amount in front of the player close to the pot. Then proceed as above directly in front of the player, placing the last two chips on top of the stacks of five, but offset. If there are more than two odd chips, it is better to spread them on the table. Announce the amount of change given (e.g., "seventeen change"). Be sure the bill goes in the well (inside the rack); you can straighten it later when you have both hands free. Keep the bills in the rack in sorted order so it's easy for the next dealer to count the bank.

If the change you counted out is not close enough to the player for him to pick it up easily then you should restack it, keeping only your index finger on top, and pass it to him.

Mechanical Skill No. 11: Opening rolled coins. Quarter or half-dollar rolls often must be opened while a hand is in progress without slowing the action. You must learn to do this with only one hand while staying completely focused on the action. Strike one end of the roll sharply against a corner of the rack to break the paper, then push the coins out from the other end directly into the coin row of the rack. Learn to do it with one hand so you don't roll the deck.

Never have more than one roll at a time open in your rack. (See "The Dealer's Rack.")

Mechanical Skill No. 12: Pot appearance. Pots that appear large are a desirable characteristic of poker. Large pots have the "illusion of action" and most players like an "action-packed game." Large pots also result in the maximum rake for the house and frequently a "big toke" for the dealer. Of course, you, the dealer have no control over the player's actual betting action, but you can help to stimulate the action by allowing the pot to appear as big as possible.

Specifically, do not gather the pot into a tight pile, and don't stack the chips unless it is required for a high-low split game. Keep the pot clear of the rack and all players. Never comment on the size of the pot, not only will this irritate the loser(s), but it will frequently irritate the winner as well since he may view your comment as an attempt to "hustle a toke."

Holding the Deck

The following instructions assume that you are righthanded. If you will be pitching lefthanded, interchange the words "left" and "right" in the following text. Better yet, learn to deal righthanded if possible. (There are no lefthanded blackjack dealers in Las Vegas.). The table is set up for right handers, making some things a bit awkward for a lefthanded dealer.

1. Hold the deck so it feels comfortable in your left hand. One corner of the deck should be placed in the crease at the base of your thumb so that the thumb is completely free to slide the top card off the deck to the side.

2. Your left index finger should be out of the way near the lower right corner of the deck at whatever position allows for the easiest pitch, but it must not be higher than the top edge of the deck.

3. Place the other three fingers on the side even with the top of the deck or just slightly above the top of the deck. You might want to put the bottom edge of the deck in or just above the crease of the first joint of these fingers. There should be a gap of about 3/4 inch between your middle finger and the front corner of the deck.

4. Be sure to keep the deck level at all times. The deck must *never* be turned over ("rolled") while a hand is in progress. (This means do not look at your watch unless it is on your other wrist.) You may say "The bottom of the deck is covered, so a card can't be exposed. Why is it so important not to roll the deck?" The answer is that you should avoid any suspicion that you may be peeking at the top card as you bring the inverted deck close to the rack.

5. Keep the deck squared so that a card cannot be exposed, but never cover the top of the deck with your other hand to square it up. (A player might suspect you of placing a palmed card on top of the deck). Instead, just moving around the fingers of your left hand will usually square up the deck. If

it's really necessary to square it up front to back, put your left index finger up the front of the deck, and tap the back end with the thumb or knuckle of your right hand.

6. Never pull a card off the deck with your right hand, and never take a card off the back of the deck. Always push it off the side first with your left thumb and grasp it at the front corner. This is to avoid any suspicion that you may be dealing "seconds" or "bottoms."

7. When you finish dealing a round of cards, go to "idle" position. Let your deck hand relax, and rest both hands at the sides of the rack clearly visible but not blocking the view of the first or last seat, while keeping the deck level. When it is time to deal the next card, have the deck up in your left hand to the correct pitching position.

8. Drop the deck in a short slide at the completion of the deal — always leaving the stub of the deck retrievable should it be necessary to correct any irregularity on the deal. Drop the cut card on or near the muck, never leave it in front of the player in the first or last seat.

Pitching Down Cards

You don't just deal the cards. In poker there is a correct way to "pitch," and it is different from what blackjack dealers are required to do in the pit. This is because in poker down cards are "private cards" and should only be seen by the player they are intended for.[24] The procedures are as follows.

1. Sit up straight. Reach out so that your arms are fairly straight and sloped down from the shoulders to your hands, and *keep your wrists straight and close together.* Holding the deck as described previously, rest the knuckles of the fourth and fifth fingers of both hands lightly against the table. Your arms and elbows should not be touching the table. The deck should be sloped slightly downward in front but not tilted to the left or right.

2. Use your left thumb to rotate the top card to the right (not forward) about ½ inch. Your thumb tip should end up just above the tip of your middle finger so that your middle finger keeps the second card from moving with the top card. Simultaneously, bring your right hand in so that the index finger touches the side of the deck at the front corner (that is, into the gap described in step 3 of "Holding the Deck").

3. With your right thumb directly above the tip of your index finger, grasp the corner of the card, but *do not lift it off of the deck.* Check to be sure that the card isn't bent.

   A common error is to have your thumb too far back so that it bends the card downward behind the index finger. Another common error is to apply upward pressure with the fingers of the left hand, thus bending the card. Bending

---

[24]The river card should be pitched — not placed and slid — to the player. Although there are a few cardrooms that prefer the latter method.

the card will cause it to wobble in the air and possibly flash or flip over.

4. Extend the middle finger of your right hand straight out to the table with a quick, smooth stroke, thus propelling the card forward while using the top of the deck as a launching ramp. Follow through; the tip of your middle finger should end up touching the table. The card should travel in the direction that the deck is aimed, touch the table about half way to the destination, and slide the rest of the way.

   Don't let the fourth or fifth fingers of your right hand interfere with a good pitch. If they are getting in the way, try practicing while holding a chip in the palm of your right hand with those two fingers. Also, remember that it is all finger motion. No wrist motion is needed to pitch the cards. Yes, some dealers are quite fast using a wrist pitch, but you will eventually be faster if you learn a good finger pitch.[25]

5. Repeat steps 1 through 4 to pitch the next card. Always point the deck where you want the card to go before pitching it. For initial practice, continue pitching to the same spot directly across the table. Pitching to various seats around the table will come later.

6. The next step in pitching practice is to go to two spots directly across the table. Swing both hands together, keeping your wrists parallel, so the deck is pointed toward the destination *before* each card is pitched, still using the top of the deck as a launching ramp. When you are comfortable with two spots, go

---

[25]Do your wrists hurt, or do your fingers tingle? These could be symptoms of carpal tunnel syndrome, an inflammation of the tendons and nerves that pass through a channel of your wrist bones. Irritation is caused by repeated wrist movement or by repeated finger movement with your wrist bent. Check with your doctor. To avoid this potentially painful problem, learn to keep your wrists straight while pitching cards.

to four spots, then to six. This requires a wider swing, but don't pivot your back that much; instead, bring your left elbow to your side to swing left, reach out as you move to the right, and bring your right elbow back as you swing to the right. Don't go beyond six spots (four on a stud table) without modifying the technique as in the next step.

7. Assuming a ten seat-table, start with the deck pointed at seat three. Carry a card forward off the deck, turn your wrist to the left (not too sharply), and use the same middle finger stroke to gently pitch to seat one. Repeat for seat two but using a full finger stroke. Seat two may need a lot of practice, as it is usually the hardest for a righthanded dealer to pitch to, especially if the player in seat one is leaning over the table. Then pitch to seats three through eight as described in step 6 above. Stop moving the deck at seat eight, and turn your wrist back slightly to pitch to seats nine and ten. Your knuckles should be kept close to the table for all of this. Important: Be sure to carry the deck all the way back to point to seat three before taking the card off for seat one.

Assuming there is no table available to practice on, a good exercise to use at home is to pitch cards into a hat or bowl to develop accuracy.

Pitching Problems

Many new dealers have a problem with down cards being exposed because they wobble or flip over. If you have this problem, it is probably due to one or more of the following common technique errors:

1. You may be throwing the card with a wrist motion instead of pitching with your fingers only. This is by far the most common error. It is not only poor technique, but it will eventually limit your speed in getting out hands, and it could lead to carpal tunnel syndrome (see preceding section). Learn the finger pitch.

2. The thumb of your pitching hand may not be at the very front corner of the card. If it is behind your index finger instead of directly above it, the front edge of the card will be bent upward, causing it to catch air and flip over.

3. You may be lifting the card off the deck before pitching. Instead, you should utilize the top of the deck as a launching ramp. A "swish" should be heard as each card slides off the deck.

4. The deck may be sloped up in front. This causes you either to pitch upward or to bend the card down over the front of the deck. The deck should be pointed to a spot on the table about halfway to the destination.[26]

5. The middle finger of your pitching hand may be under the card instead of against the edge of the card. This will flip the card up instead of propelling it straight forward.

6. You may not be following through with the middle finger. Lay the backs of both hands lightly on the table and sight over the corner of the deck to a spot on the table. Think of

---

[26]Blackjack dealers are generally required to slope the deck up. In poker, because down cards need to remain private, it is the opposite.

that spot as your target. After each card is pitched, your middle finger should be straight out with the tip touching the table at that target spot. Use a smooth stroke with complete follow-through, as in "stroking the cue ball" in pool. A golf or tennis swing is similar, requiring a smooth follow-through for good control of the ball.

7. The fingers of your deck hand may be too high above the edge of the deck, so the card is bent when it is pushed off.

8. You may be resting your elbows or forearms on the table instead of reaching out and resting your knuckles lightly on the table.

9. A fan, air conditioner, or open door may be causing a breeze across the table. Usually this will cause a problem only in one area of the table. Just be particularly careful to pitch the cards low on the table.

Pitching Up Cards

While dealing up cards is not as crucial as down cards, their order and placement must be accurate. Though it is up to the players to keep their cards in order (by streets) it is up to the dealer to pitch the cards so that they land in the proper sequence. The procedures are as follows.

1. Holding the deck as described earlier, keep the knuckles of both hands down as if to touch the table as you did to pitch down cards, but hold your hands about four to six inches above the table. The deck should always be level.

2. Bring your right hand in so that the thumb, nail up, enters the gap in front of the middle finger of your left hand. Simultaneously, use your left thumb to slide the top card to the right about 1 inch.

3. Place your right index finger on top of the card above your thumbnail and your right middle finger on the front edge of the card.

4. Raise your right thumb and roll it up and over your index finger. Simultaneously, follow the front edge of the card around with your middle finger. The card will flip over, back to front, and should now be nearly level and about 1 inch higher than the top of the deck.

   You should now be holding the card with your right thumb directly over the index finger. Your knuckles are still down, and your right middle finger tip is close to the base of your thumb and directly behind the back end of the card.

5. Propel the card forward with your middle finger, just as for pitching down cards except that you are pitching it slightly upward through the air instead of down against the table. With the right amount of thrust, it will fall flat in the desired position and not slide significantly. It is important that up cards stop where they land without sliding so you can place them in small groups.

As in the down card pitch, it is all finger motion. No wrist motion or rotation is required to pitch the cards.

Burning a Card

Before each succeeding round of cards after the betting is complete, it is required that the top card be "burned" or discarded. This is done to assure the integrity of the game. The proper procedures are as follows.

1. Always tap the table before you burn. This is to notify the players of your intent so that they can stop your action should the betting be incomplete.
2. Hold the deck as for pitching a down card, with the deck aimed where you are going to place the burn card.
3. Push the top card off with your left thumb, and place your right index finger on the top right corner of the card pointing straight ahead. Grasp the edge of the card with your right thumb and middle finger (or fourth finger), and slide the card *forward* off the deck.
4. Place the card on the table, and tuck it under the pot or previous burn card(s) where it can be seen.
5. Each additional burn card should be tucked under the previous one. Form a staggered pattern so anyone can see at a glance how many burn cards there are at any time.
6. Always leave the burn cards under the edge of the pot until it is pushed. Clean burn cards may be *essential*.
7. It is important that the burn card is not exposed. However, if it does flash or turn over then it must be shown to all active players.

Spreading the Flop

The second round of cards in hold 'em or Omaha are also dealt up, but the procedure is totally different since these cards, known as the "flop," are community cards. An incorrect flop can be a source of major contention since many hands are affected at the same time. The following steps need to be followed precisely as described.

1. Be sure the pot is positioned so there is room for the community cards in the very center of the table.
2. Hold the deck low, in front of the rack where you should have clear space to place the flop. Tap the table and burn a card under the edge of the pot as described previously. Count three cards off the deck one at a time onto the table.
3. Using your right hand, press lightly on the right edge of the cards with your fingertips to lift the left edge. Get your thumb underneath. Stand the cards up on edge against your middle finger.
4. As you reach out to where you want to spread the flop, square them with your index finger. Position your thumb at the center of the left edge of the cards so that it protrudes beyond the edge of the cards. Your thumb tip should touch the table first. Just open your hand to drop the cards and spread with only the soft part of your thumb tip. Don't lay your hand down on the cards. Be sure to expose all flop cards at once.
5. The first card should line up with the left edge of the rack and stay where it's dropped as the other two slide to the right. (If you're dealing lefthanded, you will drop and spread from the middle to the left.)
6. All flop cards should be exposed to all the players at the same time, so move your hand out of the way quickly. Use just your fingertips to straighten up the flop. Ideally, there should be about ¼ inch to ½ inch of space between the cards.

Splitting a Pot

Although splitting a pot is most frequently required in high-low split games, it is also necessary in straight high or straight low games when two or more players have equivalent hands. (For example, two stud players each have a jack-high straight, or two hold 'em players are playing the board).[27]

1. If it is a high-low split flop game, keep the pot behind the board cards instead of to the left or in front of the flop, but not too close to the rack (at least 2 inches of clear space).
2. Don't delay the game by stacking all the chips after each betting round. Pull the bets in, burn and turn the next card, and get the action going.
3. Stack the chips during the hand as time permits, but don't lose sight of the action. You must continue to announce bets, raises, and so forth, as usual, and stay focused on the game.
4. Create two side-by-side stacks of each chip denomination, with the higher denomination chips in front. If it's a large pot you will have several stacks of chips. But don't worry about making the stacks equal until the showdown.
5. At the end of the action, pull all bets in, and begin reading hands. Don't delay by finishing the stacking, as it's not always necessary to split the pot.
6. If there is only one winner, push the entire pot; it's not necessary to finish stacking the pot, but don't inconvenience the winner by knocking over any chips you already had stacked. Otherwise, finish stacking the pot once the winners have been determined. Make sure the stacks are equal, and push them to the winners, pushing the higher denomination

---

[27]It is rare for two players in a stud game to have hands of the exact same value. However, in flop games like hold 'em and Omaha these types of hands can occur several times an hour.

chips first. Don't put coins on top of a tall stack of chips; it's too hard to control such a stack.

7. If there is a tie for one or both ends of the pot, first split the pot into two equal halves for high and low. If there is only one winner for either half, push that half, and muck that winning hand unless that hand is also getting part of the other half of the pot. Finally, restack the remaining half to divide as necessary between the tied winners for that end of the pot. There's no need to count the pot. For a three-way tie, simply make three equal stacks.

8. An odd chip usually goes to the high hand. If the high end or low end is split, an odd chip usually goes to the first player left of the button. In some rooms, however, the dealer keeps the odd chip as a toke. (However, don't do this unless you're sure it is the policy in your room.)

Getting a Fill

Unlike pit games, a poker dealer's rack always contains a fixed amount of chips and cash. It is used strictly for changing players' money into chips and coins for convenient betting and rake purposes. Whenever chips or money leave the bank, an equal amount must go in. The procedure for getting a fill is as follows:

1. Call for a fill by table number (e.g., "Fill on three") when you have less than two full stacks of required chips or coins.[28] The best time to call for a fill is when you are about halfway through a hand so the chiprunner can be there when the hand finishes.

2. Do not hold up the game waiting for a fill. If the chiprunner has not arrived by the time you're ready to deal the next hand, call again for a fill, but go ahead and deal.

3. When the chiprunner arrives and the hand in progress is finished, take the cash and excess high denomination chips from the rack and count it down out loud on the table in full view.

4. The total is verified by the chiprunner. Lammers representing that amount are placed on the table, and the dealer hands the money from the table to the chiprunner. A good place for the lammers is between the rack and the drop slot.[29]

---

[28]This might mean quarters in a $1-$3 game or $25 chips in a $75-$150 game.

[29]Lammers are left on the table when getting a fill to show how much is temporarily missing from the rack so that the effective total does not change. (This is required by gaming regulations in Nevada.) In some cardrooms the chiprunner carries lammers and leaves the proper amount. In others the lammers are in the rack, and the dealer puts out the correct amount. (The latter is more likely in a room that does not have an employee whose primary duty is

5. Tell the chiprunner how much is needed of each denomination. Typically you might indicate the amount needed in $5 chips, $1 chips, and the number of rolls of coins. For example, "200 red, 60 blue, and 4 halves" would mean $200 in red chips, $60 in blue chips, and four rolls of half dollars.

6. The chiprunner gets the fill, returns to the table, and waits until the hand in progress is finished. When the dealer is ready, the chip rack(s) containing the fill are placed on the table. The dealer counts it down to verify the amount by breaking down one full stack of each color and any short stacks to verify that the amount of chips is correct. Then, and only then, is it put in the rack.

7. If the lammers are not kept in the dealer's rack, they are put in the empty chip rack and handed to the chiprunner. The chiprunner should not pick up the lammers. Any trash (e.g., empty coin wrappers) may also be put in the empty chip rack for disposal. Do not throw coin wrappers on the floor.

8. **Foreign chips,** that is chips from another casino, should never be taken into the rack. Foreign chips are chips or tokens brought to the game by players from other casinos, sports books, baccarat, and so on. They are to be changed up immediately by a chiprunner or floorperson as they cannot legally play in the game.

---

primary duty is running chips; instead, a floorperson or a dealer on break gets the fill.) Lammers usually have standard colors: brown, $100; yellow, $50; pink, $25; blue, $20; red, $10; beige or white, $5. Many cardrooms do not use $25 or $50 lammers.

Button and Blind Rules

At first glance it may appear as if the section devoted to the button and blinds is very long, out of proportion, in fact. But there are many variations in regulations and house policy regarding the button and blinds, plus certain situations can complicate matters even more. It would be nearly impossible to cover all variations and exceptions, but we will attempt to discuss the most common ones.

The word "button" when used alone refers specifically to the dealer button (as opposed to missed blind buttons, etc.). See "Other Buttons" for a discussion of other cases where the word "button" is used.

In this book we use the terms "after" meaning "clockwise from" and "before" meaning "counterclockwise from" when looking down upon the table. The terms "left" and "right" are avoided because there can be some confusion as to whether it refers to the player's left or the dealer's left.

Most of the rules regarding the blinds and missed blinds will make more sense if you think of the blinds as payment *in advance* to see one round of hands. It is not necessary for a player to make up a blind for hands that he did not receive, but if he missed one or more blinds and wants to play before the blinds come around to him again, then he must pay to look at those remaining hands in the current round.

Nevada Button Rules

Following are the most common rules and variations that you are likely to encounter in cardrooms in Nevada.[30]

General

A player may receive a hand "on the button" (in the seat where the button is positioned) only if he posted all blinds in sequence as they came to him. The principal exception is when starting a new game. (See "Starting a New Game.") However, there are some rooms that allow a player who missed a blind to make it up on the button.

You should announce "dead button" when starting to deal if the seat where the button is positioned is not receiving a hand. This can occur if the player missed one or more blinds and must wait for the button to pass, if the player left the table or said to deal him out, or if the player now in that seat is not the same one who posted the blinds.

Single Blind

The button moves to the *seat* that posted the blind on the previous hand. The word "seat" is emphasized because moving the button past that seat to the next active player would mean that the player receiving the button had not paid a blind. If the seat with the button isn't receiving a hand for any reason, you should announce "dead button" as you start to deal.

---

[30] At the time of this writing, most of the cardrooms of Northern Nevada are using the "Advancing Button Rules," which are discussed on page 95.

91

The blind is posted by the first active player after the dealer button. There can never be a dead blind.

Any player not present, but whose chips are between the button and the blind gets a "missed blind" button. This occurs when the player who would have had the blind left the table or asked to be dealt out.

If a new player sits down in the blind position, he may have the option to wait until the button passes, in which case he gets to play his first round of hands without paying a blind. In many rooms, however, he will receive a missed blind button if he doesn't take the blind immediately. (See "The No Free Hands Rule" on page 98.)

Two Blinds

The button moves to the *seat* that was *designated* the small blind last hand. The two emphasized words are important because it doesn't matter whether or not that blind was actually paid or what player (if any) is currently in that seat. The player in the seat with the button can't receive a hand, however, unless that same player paid all blinds in sequence as they came to him. If that seat isn't receiving a hand for any reason, you should announce "dead button" as you start to deal.

The small blind goes to the seat that posted the big blind last hand. That seat can receive a hand only if the same player who posted the big blind is still there and posts the small blind. If that seat isn't receiving a hand for any reason, you should announce "no small blind" and, unless the player who posted the big blind last hand has left the game, you should toss a "Small Blind" button to that seat.

The big blind goes to the first active player after the small blind. Any player between the small blind and big blind who isn't receiving a hand gets a "big blind" button. (The exception is a new player who hasn't yet received a hand, and then only if the "no free hands" rule is *not* in effect.) There can never be a dead big blind.

If there are more than two blinds, the above discussion works if you think of it as one big blind and two or more small blinds.

Missed Blinds
(Nevada Button Rules)

No player can receive a hand between the button and the blinds. If a new player sits down in a seat that is between the button and the small blind(s), he has no choice but to wait for the button to pass, so a missed blind button is not necessary. In some rooms, however, he will be required to post a big blind for his first hand after the button passes. (See "The No Free Hands Rule.")

No player can receive a hand on the button unless he paid all blinds in sequence as they came to him. The player may come back in at any time after the button passes by making up all missed blinds, or he may wait for the big blind to reach his seat.

Returning without Making up the Blinds

A player who missed one or more blinds may simply wait for the big blind to come to him again, and there is no need to make up missed blinds. The reason for this is clear if you think of the blinds as payment *in advance* to see the next round of hands.

Missed Small Blind

After the button passes, the player may come back in by posting an amount equal to the small blind. When the action reaches him, he has the option to call by making up the difference between the blind posted and the current bet (same as for the regular small blind). In some rooms, this "out-of-position" small blind is considered dead. That is, the player posting a dead blind cannot call unless he puts in the amount of a full bet. In most rooms, the small blind is "dead" if missed and "live" if a player changes seats when the small blind is due.

Missed Big Blind

After the button passes, the player may come back in by posting an amount equal to the sum of the small and big blinds. (It is impossible to miss only the big blind since once a blind is missed the player must wait for the button to pass.)

The dealer takes the small blind portion into the center of the table. This is "dead money." It is not part of the player's live blind, but it is counted as part of the pot for the purpose of calculating the rake.

The big blind portion is live; when the action gets to that player, the dealer should say "option" and treat it the same as a regular big blind.

Missed Blind in a Single Blind Game

After the button passes, the player may come back in by posting a blind equal to the regular blind. The blind is live; when the action gets to that player, the dealer should say "option" and treat it the same as the regular blind.

The player also has the option to wait until the blind reaches him; then no make-up blind is required.

Advancing Button Rule
(Not Common in Nevada)

The Advancing Button Rule is used in California and some other jurisdictions. When this rule is in effect, the button never stops at a seat that will not be receiving a hand but always advances to the next active player.

The purpose is to avoid a dead button, which makes the same player last to act two hands in a row. It is obviously unfair to allow one player to be last to act two hands in a row when the other players get the button only once per round. It is not a big increase in advantage, however, because that player would be next-to-last anyway if the button advances.

The advancing button method is not completely fair either because the next player gets to pay the blind in the favorable position of being on the button instead of "under the gun." But if you will be dealing in a jurisdiction that uses this rule you will be required to know how to implement it, so...

Single Blind

The button always advances to the next active player, bypassing any empty seats or players who for any reason will not be receiving a hand. If it moves to a player who has not yet posted the blind, there will be two blinds this hand — one on the button, and the next active player.

Two Blinds

The small blind moves to the button, and there will be two big blinds after the button. The next hand the button advances, the player on the button will post a small blind, the player after him will post a small blind, the next player has a big blind. (Note: There will always be two blinds after the button.)

It gets even more complicated when two or more players miss their blinds and return at the same time. It is our opinion (and apparently that of most cardroom managers in Nevada) that the slight gain in fairness is not worth the complications added by the advancing button rule.

Dealer Actions
for Missed Blinds

Most of the actions required of the dealer are the same with either button rule. When the action reaches a player with a "make-up" blind you should make the same announcement you would for the regular blind of the same size (assuming the make-up blind is live money). That is, say "Option" or "Dead blind."

It would be redundant to give a small blind button to a seat that already has a big blind button since it is impossible to miss only the big blind. If a seat already has a small blind button from an earlier round and then misses the big blind, it is optional to retrieve the small blind button when giving the big blind button.

It is suggested that you leave the missed blind button next to a player's make-up blind until that player acts in turn; this reminds you that the situation there is different. Consider in particular, the case where seat one missed the big blind, and the button is at seat seven. You deal the cards, and since seats eight and nine have posted blinds you look to seat ten for his action, then turn your head and see that seat one already has a bet in front of him. If you don't remember that it's a make-up blind, you may forget to give that player his option. (However, in medium- and high-limit games this is rarely done; the players will usually wait for the blinds to "come around.")

Even with the Nevada button rules, some cardrooms allow making up a missed blind on the button. Of course this contradicts some of the things said on the preceding pages, and some rooms handle it differently than others, so you must find out from your supervisor exactly what the correct procedure is.

The No Free Hands Rule

The no free hands rule is nearly always in effect when following the advancing button rule, and it is often in effect when following the Nevada button rule in a room that spreads any high-limit games.

A new player must post or wait for the big blind. Of course if he happens to be between the button and the small blind he must wait one hand and post the big blind behind the button.

A new player always has the option to wait for the big blind. (Some cardrooms allow a new player to let the blinds pass and then post the big blind only, behind the button.)

Starting a New Game

When starting a new game, the button must start somewhere. In this case, someone is going to receive a hand on the button without having posted any blinds. Also, if there are two or more blinds, one or more players will be getting the button without having posted all of the blinds.

Some rooms always start the button in seat ten so that the deal starts at seat one. The result is that some players try to get a late position seat to start the game so they get several free hands.

A more fair and equitable way of assigning the button is to have the players draw cards from a shuffled and spread deck. The player who draws the highest card by rank and suit is awarded the dealer's position.

Starting the button in seat ten would be fine in a tournament since the seats are randomly assigned, yet many tournaments are started by drawing for the button. This seems to be a waste of time.

Players Changing Seats

Players frequently change seats at the table. When a player leaves the game, any other player in the game generally has the option to move to the vacant seat before a new player sits down.

If a player moves toward the blinds, there is no problem. If he is moving away from the blinds, however, then cardroom policy may require that he post an extra blind or sit out a number of hands equal to the number of seats he has moved. In some rooms a player is allowed to move one or two seats away from the button without penalty. Ask the floorperson if you're not sure whether a make-up blind is required.

If a player simply slides over one or more vacant seats this does not change his position relative to the other players, so it has no affect on blinds, and so forth. If such a player has the button or a blind, it simply moves with the player.

Players Changing Tables

Players often move or "transfer" from one game to another. If the move is at the player's option he is generally treated the same as a new player entering the game. If the no free hands rule is in effect he will be required to post a big blind immediately or wait until it is his turn to take the big blind. However, he probably is not required to post a new player blind if he is coming from a broken game of the same type and limit and will be dealt in immediately. Ask the floorperson if you're not sure whether a blind is required.

Any player already in the game generally has first option to move to a vacant seat. (See "Players Changing Seats" in the preceding section.)

All players are required to have at least a full buy-in to voluntarily change tables. Broken games however allow you to sit with any amount of money remaining.

Other Buttons

Several other types of buttons may be used, such as:

1. **Reserved button.** Indicates that a seat is being held for a specific new player, a returning player, or that the seat is locked up to keep the number of players equal in two separate games.

2. **Absent button.** When you first enter the box, toss an absent button to each seat where there are chips but no player. An accumulation of two or three absent buttons at the same seat indicates that the player has been gone about an hour.[31] Call the floorperson if a player has been away from the table over the maximum allowed time.

3. **Generic button.** Some rooms do not use any labeled buttons other than the dealer button. Blank chips are used for all of the above situations. This is false savings because it leaves some situations unclear, especially when changing dealers.

4. **Kill button.** In some games there may be situations where a pot is "killed." The presence of the kill button in the pot shows that the betting limits are doubled for that one hand. In lowball draw, any player may be allowed to kill the pot after looking at his first two cards by saying "kill" and posting a double size blind.[32] In other games, a player may be required to kill the next pot after winning two hands in a row or when scooping the pot in a high-low split game. Some rooms have a "half kill" meaning that the limits go up 50 percent instead of being

---

[31]Two absent buttons represent an hour in those cardrooms where the dealer has thirty minute downs. Three absent buttons represent an hour in those cardrooms where the dealer has twenty minute downs.

[32]A small number of cardrooms allow "look-at-three" and kill.

doubled and have qualifiers on the pot size before a kill is posted.[33]

---

[33]For example, providing the previously scooped pot reached at least $50, a $10-$20 game becomes $15-$30 for the next hand.

The Sequence of Events

Many students think, "I know poker. All I have to do is learn to shuffle and pitch cards, and I'll be a poker dealer." However, there is much more that needs to be done to run the game correctly. Following is the general sequence of events to complete a hand.

1. Scramble and call "Antes please,"and/or "Blinds please," as required.
2. Shuffle, box, shuffle, shuffle. (See "Mechanical Skills" on page 69.)[34]
3. Position the cut card, and release the deck.
4. Gather the antes, if any, into the center of the table, making change as necessary.
5. Cut the cards — with one hand. (See "Mechanical Skills" on page 69.) If necessary, square the deck on the table before picking it up.
6. Place the deck in your hand. (See "Holding the Deck" on page 75.)
7. Deal the cards. (See "Pitching Down Cards," "Pitching Problems" and "Pitching Up Cards" on pages 77, 80, and 82 respectively.) Once the last card for that round has been dealt, your attention should immediately be on the player who is first to act, and you should be in rest position.[35]

---

[34]Most cardrooms use a mini-scramble before every shuffle. A full scramble is used whenever the set-up and/or deck is changed.

[35]"Rest position" is sitting erect with your hands at the sides of the bank and your elbows at your sides. Let your deck hand rest on its back so the deck always remains level.

8. Start the action, using an open hand, and announce all bets and raises. Always speak out clearly so that all players can hear. A dealer should always be in control of the game. However, you should not overcall the game. (It's generally not necessary to announce every check or every call.)
9. Make sure that the blinds get their options.
10. If a player folds, slide the discards immediately into the muck. The discards *should* always be *slid,* never lifted, so that a player's discarded hand is not accidentally exposed. Never place anything on top of the muck, and do not square up the muck or "massage" the muck.
11. After betting is complete on each round, bring in all bets using both hands. Be careful to keep the deck level. Extend only the little finger or middle finger of your deck hand and lay the back of your hand on the table to give a wide area for sweeping in chips.
12. As you bring in the bets you should determine the number of players and the new total in the pot, thus calculating the rake. After you have dealt the next round of cards take your rake.
13. Repeat steps 8 through 13 until all betting rounds have been completed, except that before dealing each additional round of cards or putting up board cards:
    a. You should tap the table. This is a signal that you are about to deal thus enabling the players to stop your action in case the betting is incomplete.
    b. The top card off the deck must be burned. (See "Burning a Card" on page 84.) This is to protect the deck.
    c. In hold 'em or other flop games, announce the number of active players and any all-in players (e.g., "Four players, one all-in"). In stud it is not necessary to announce the number of players since the up cards identify who is still in the hand, but you should announce any all-in players.
    d. Before dealing the last card to a full table in seven-card stud, be sure you have enough cards. (See "Checking for Enough Cards" on page 139.)

14. After dealing the last round and starting the action, drop the deck in a short slide. Count the stub of the deck at least once per down. (See "Stub Counts" on page 151.)

15. When all the action is completed, ask the players to show their hands, if necessary. If the hand is checked and everyone hesitates then the hands are usually shown down in the same order as the betting action. Remember, if a bettor is called, the bettor must show first. Read any hand as soon as it's shown, but do not attempt to read a hand until the player turns up all his cards, and never turn up any player's cards on your own.

16. Read all hands, killing each losing hand individually by turning it face down and sliding it into the muck.[36] Never put any hand on top of the muck. Leave only the winning hand(s) face-up on the table.

    Don't let the players rush you. When several hands are turned up simultaneously, the players will read some of them before you do. They are usually right, but they can make mistakes, too. You alone are responsible for pushing the pot to the player with the best hand. If you make an error, depending on house policy, it could be your loss.

17. After determining the winning hand and mucking all losing hands:

    a. Push the pot to the winner, and bring your hands back palms-up;

---

[36]The first and perhaps only universal rule of poker is that each player must protect his own hand. However, you should not deprive a player of the right to do so by grabbing a hand and mucking it without warning. Turning the cards face down in front of the player gives the player time to call out or grab your hand before the cards get to the muck. In such a case, you should turn the cards back up and read the hand again. Once the cards reach the muck, however, they should be slid into the side of the muck so that they are unidentifiable.

b. Move the dealer button;[37]
c. Drop the rake; and
d. Muck the winning hand and start to scramble for the next hand.

The winning hand is mucked last, after everything else is done. Push the pot — move the button. Remember, all this will come naturally to the professional.

Repeat the entire sequence from the top for the next hand. Other than the required announcements, you should never make any comment or show any reaction to the board cards, to any player's cards, or to the way a player plays a hand.

When a player tosses you a toke, say "Thank you," and try to make eye contact immediately even if you will not be picking it up until after the shuffle. (Sometimes a player will toss you a toke before a hand is over. When that is the case, say "Thank you," and pick up the toke immediately, lightly tapping the edge of the rack before putting it in your pocket.)

Note: In any game with antes, tokes are to be picked up *before* bringing in the antes.

---

[37]If the button is in front of the winner, it may be pushed first to get it out of the way.

Calling the Action — Texas Hold 'em or Omaha

Blinds

Call for the blinds while shuffling. Since you have mastered a complete shuffle without watching your hands, you can point with your eyes.

If a player does not post his required blind, "Blinds, please" is the only acceptable way to request that he comply. Call twice, if a player does not respond and is *clearly* not being distracted, give him a missed blind button and request the blind from the next person.

Immediately after dealing the last card to the button, look — never stare — at the first player after the big blind. If that player has not yet acted, you can just say "Ten to call," (or whatever the amount of the big blind). It's usually not necessary to give a hand signal, as most players will look up at the dealer's face when any such announcement is made to see whom you're talking to. Point with your eyes, not your finger, or use an open hand.

During Later Rounds

Announce the number of players as you bring in the bets at the end of each betting round.

Immediately after spreading the flop or putting up the turn or river card, you should be looking at the first active player after the button. Never make any comment or show any reaction to the board cards.

In a Medium- or High-Stakes Game

Announce bets and raises only. If the action stalls, you should say to the first player "It's up to you" or you may use an open hand (only if the player seems unaware it is on him to act). If a player is obviously thinking about his action then it is better to call "time."

Calling the Action —
Seven-Card Stud

Antes

In games that require an ante, call for the antes while shuffling. If a player does not post his required ante, "Antes, please" is the only acceptable way to request that he comply. Call twice, if a player does not respond and is *clearly* not being distracted give him a reserved (yellow) button to make him aware that he is about to be dealt out. If there is still no response, deal around him for that hand.

In games with no antes, make an obvious release of the deck before cutting the cards. Then proceed with dealing the hand.

Bring-in

Watch as you deal out each player's door card, remembering the lowest card you've seen so far. That way you don't have to look back after dealing to the last player to see who has the bring-in. If the deuce of clubs shows it can be announced immediately since no card is lower.

Always call the low card by name and suit even if there is only one card of that rank. This way the player who is responsible for the bring-in will react quickly since he will know it is his hand. If more than one card of the same rank appears and that rank is low, remember that you announce by suit alphabetically. (For example, if there is a four of hearts and a four of diamonds the announcement would be "Four of diamonds" since diamonds precedes hearts alphabetically.)

During the Later Rounds — Low Limit

When calling any hand without a pair, call the high card by rank and suit. Announce all pairs, two pair, or three-of-a-kind as they appear. Notice the cards as they land, rather than look at each individual card as it comes off the deck. This makes it easier to recognize such improvements and it is faster.

Announce the highest hand showing as first to act. If that player is all-in then the action goes to the next player clockwise around the table. It does not go to the second highest hand. To make it easy, just think of it as being the same as if the player having the highest hand had checked.

When dealing the fourth upcard (sixth street), announce any "possible flush" (any four cards of the same suit) or "possible straight" (any four cards in sequence or with only one gap such as 4-5-6-8) as it appears. Don't wait until after dealing to the last player to announce possible straights and flushes. A hand missing only one card to make a straight flush or royal flush should be announced as "possible flush, possible straight." To announce it as a possible straight flush would imply that you had somehow determined that the specific missing card is still available.

Announce which hand is first to act as you start to deal the last card. Since this card is dealt face down it is impossible for a different player to become first to act.

In a Medium- or High-Stakes Game

Announce only which player is first to act. Do not announce possible straights or flushes. If the action stalls, you should announce which hand is next to act *only if the player seems unaware of the fact that it is his turn to act*. If a player is obviously thinking about his action, it's better to call "time."

Controlling the Action

Shuffling and dealing the cards is only the beginning of a dealer's job. Your most important responsibility is running your game, also known as controlling the action.

Except for a stud game with a 50¢ bring-in, or when a player goes all-in and includes quarters that are not a multiple of four (where this is allowed), all bets are in whole dollars.[38] Thus it's not necessary to announce "Three dollars" when a player puts out three blue chips. "Three" is enough to get the message across.

If the next player raises three dollars, announce "Raise, make it six." Your first word should always be "raise," and it should be immediate.

If a player puts the chips out in a tall stack or a messy pile so that you have to reach out and count them, you should announce "Raise" immediately, and continue with "make it [*whatever the amount*]" after you have counted the chips. This deters further action until the amount is known. This is especially important if the player in the seat to the dealer's right puts out a raise without an announcement, as the player in seat one may not see the raise. The action might continue with calls of the original bet if you don't announce "raise" immediately.

Along with the word "raise" you have stated the amount of the total bet, so it is usually not necessary to say any more to the next player. When you get back to the original bettor, you should announce "three to call" (or whatever amount is required).

---

[38]Some cardrooms now require minimum bets to be in increments of the smallest chip used for that game. For example, if a player has $12 left in a $20-$40 game he will only be allowed to bet (or call) with $10 since $5 chips are the smallest chip used in this game.

Oversize Chips or Cash

When a player puts down an oversize chip or cash with no announcement, it is presumed to be a call. You should immediately announce "Call." This is a statement, not a question. Once the money leaves the player's hand with no announcement by the player it is too late to raise.

In the low-limit games announce the action of any oversize chip or cash as it is played, but just leave it positioned in front of the player. Make change immediately whenever possible from the pot.

However, at $10-$20 or higher make change immediately marking the bet in front of the player. This will help you maintain a fast-paced game which the players at the middle- and high-limits appreciate.

If a player has, say, only a $100 bill in front of him, and there is a raise, wait until the action returns to the player with the bill. Usually just the word "Call?" as a question is enough. Of course he may want to raise, which is his option (unless there have already been the maximum number of raises). Whatever the player does, announce "That's six [or whatever the new amount] on the piece." (See "On the Piece Bets" on page 134.)

When the action is finished, and before gathering in the bets, announce the amount to be taken from the bill; for example, "Ten out of a hundred." If possible, when dealing the medium or high limits, try to make change from the pot since this will minimize the need for fills. Otherwise take a stack of chips from your rack, cut out the six close to the pot, and cut down the remaining chips in front of the player, announcing "Fourteen change." Take the bill, and put it in the well (you can straighten it later when you have both hands available). Gather in all bets as usual, and continue with the hand.

Number of Raises

Many cardrooms allow a maximum of three raises, but some allow four. You must know your room's policy and enforce it by announcing "That's the cap" or "Last raise" when the last allowed raise is made.

In a spread-limit game, the size of the raise is not significant in determining the cap. Only the number of raises is important.

In most cardrooms, a straddle bet placed before the cards are dealt is considered to be a raise for the purpose of determining when the raises have been capped. However, there are some exceptions where this bet will raise the cap.

A partial raise by an all-in player, which is less than half of the bet or raise, is not usually considered to be a raise for the purpose of determining when the raises have been capped. Also, a partial raise that is less than half of the original bet does not give the original bettor an option to reraise. He may only call. For him to be allowed to reraise, there must have been a raise of at least half of his original bet.

Completing a Bet or Raise

As with so many things in poker, the rules for completing a bet or raise depend on house policy. There may even be different rules for spread-limit and structured-limit games in the same room. Due to the lack of standards, we can only discuss typical rules and common variations here.

The concept of completing a bet or raise is most easily understood with structured limit, so we will discuss that first. Suppose a player goes all-in with a partial bet. The requirements on the next player depend upon the amount of the all-in bet or raise. If it is half or more of the structured bet size then the next player must put up exactly that amount if he wants to call; he has the option to make a full raise on top of that (unless the maximum number of raises has been reached). However, if the all-in bet or raise is less than half the structured bet size then it is considered to be only action. The options of the next player are to call the all-in amount or complete it to a full bet; he may not raise it another full bet, since he is considered to be the bettor.

In spread limits, there's no such thing as a partial bet unless the lower limit of the spread is greater than one dollar. (An example would be a $1 bet in a $2-$10 game.) A partial raise occurs when an all-in bet is less than the amount to call, plus half of the bet or last raise. Depending upon house rules, the next player may be allowed to simply call the all-in amount, complete the raise to at least the amount of the bet, call the all-in amount and make a full raise, or complete the all-in raise and make a full raise (only if the all-in raise was at least half the original bet).

Raising One's Own Bet

The question of whether a player is raising his own bet often occurs after an all-in partial raise. Suppose in a $3-$6 game, player A bets $3, player B goes all-in for $4, and one or more other players call. The increase by player B is less than half the bet, so it is not a raise; it is only action. Since no one has made a valid raise, player A may not reraise since to do so would be the same as raising his own bet; he may only call or fold.

If any other player completed the raise and/or made a full raise, then player A would of course have the option to reraise if desired. Also, if the all-in bet had been $5 it would be considered a raise since the increase was half or more of the bet, so player A could call the raise or reraise even if no other player completed the raise. However, he cannot complete the raise (to $6 in this example) and then raise on top of that.

String Bets

In a spread-limit game a situation may arise where a player puts out some chips without announcing how much he intends to bet, goes back to his stack, and puts out more chips. The dealer should push back all but the first chips and say something like "I'm sorry, sir, but that's a string bet." If he seems confused, go on to say "You must either announce the amount of your bet or put it all out in one motion."

String Raise

More frequently encountered is the string raise because it's shown frequently in the movies. For example, there has been a $1,000 bet. The next player puts out $1,000, saying "I'll see your thousand..." as he reaches back to his stack "...and raise you $3,000 more." (Remember, this is the movies.) As for a string bet, you must push back all but the call amount, and say "I'm sorry, but that's a string raise." If further explanation is necessary, continue with "To raise, you must either say 'raise' before releasing any money, or put the correct total amount of money into the pot all at one time."

Minimum Raise

Many players in low stakes games have previously played only in home games where this and the previously mentioned two situations occur frequently. For example, there is a $3 bet, and the next player puts out $5. You tell him "If you want to raise, it must be at least equal to the bet or last raise." At this point, the player still has the option to make a full $3 raise since he already had put out at least half of that amount, so you could say "You can make it six if you like." If he had put out only $4 you should push back the extra check and say "The bet was only $3." In this case, the $1 excess is less than half of the bet, so he would have lost the option to raise. The exception to the minimum raise rule is when a player is going all-in, in which case he may raise whatever amount he has left on the table (subject to the "minimum chip" rule).

In a high-stakes game, a partial bet or raise may be committed to the pot, and the player would not have the option to rescind the raise.

Reading Hands

General

When the last round of betting is complete, and two or more players remain, it is time for the showdown. The players should now turn their hands over. Occasionally one or more players will be reluctant, and you will have to politely request that they show their hands or discard them.

Many dealers have their own style of getting hesitant players to show their hands. Some are effective, while others can be annoying. However, in any game with serious players it is rarely necessary to ask to see the hands.

If all players hesitate to show their hands, then the player who was in first acting position is required to show first. (In some cardrooms, mainly in Europe, the player who made the last bet or raise is required to show first.)

Don't wait for all the players to turn up their hands. As soon as any hand is shown, go ahead and read it, announcing the value out loud. When players hesitate to show their hands, it's usually because they don't want to show unless they have a winner. (Why give information about playing style when it's not necessary?) The first player to show typically does so because he thinks he has the winner, and only a player with a better hand then shows his cards. Sometimes all the other players discard their hands when they see a better hand, and you don't have to read any other hands at all.

When several players do show their hands, read whichever is more convenient, then one more. Muck the lesser of the two (unless they tie), and repeat until all hands have been read. You will end up with only the winner's (or winners') hand showing. This way you never have to go back and read a hand a second time.

Don't move a hand from in front of a player unless you intend to muck it. Even if your only intent is to make it easier for you or the other players to see the winning hand, moving it from in front of the winner gives him a momentary uneasy feeling.

Don't handle a player's cards except as necessary to read them. If there is a hidden card, just slide the covering card aside to reveal it. But never turn up a player's card that is face down.

All of a player's cards must be shown for the hand to be readable, but the "One player to a hand rule" dictates that they should be turned up *by that player*. Anyone other than a hand's owner who turns up a card is helping that player to play his hand. It's bad enough when another player does this, but it's unforgivable if the dealer does it. Just tell the player, "I'm not allowed to read a hand until all the cards are showing."

Read a pair simply as "a pair of queens," and so forth. There is no need to announce kickers unless it becomes necessary to break a tie.

Announce two pair naming the higher pair first. For example

would be read as "Two pair, queens and eights" or "Two pair, queens over eights" or simply as "Queens-up." The words "and," "over," or "up" indicate two pair.

Announce a straight or flush with the high-end card. For example, "Jack-high straight" or "King-high flush." Two straights with the same high end would split the pot. If two flushes have the same high card, go to the next highest card to determine the winner, and so on until a difference is found. If all five cards have the same rank then they split the pot. A sixth card is never considered in poker.

Avoid nonessential phrases when reading hands. "It looks like a flush" is redundant. Just say "Flush" or perhaps "Ten-high flush." Starting with "We have..." is even worse; you (the dealer) are not part of "we" (the players), and some disgruntled loser might even get the idea that you favor the winner over him. Just announce the value of the hand. Also avoid slang terms such as "all pink."

Be diplomatic. Avoid reading a hand as "Nothing" or "Just a pair of eights." If a better hand has already been read then just pull the eights out front to show that you saw them and muck the hand. Usually it's desirable to say something, however, when mucking a hand. In such a case, something like "Straight wins" (referring to the winning hand rather than to the hand you're mucking) is best.

When reading a hand, bring the significant cards out to the front. This makes it easier for the players to see the hand as you've read it, and it makes it easier for you to look at the remaining cards to see if you've missed anything. However, don't waste time by "organizing" a hand; for example, it's not necessary or proper to put the cards of a straight in sequence. (You should handle the cards as little as possible.)

When mucking a losing hand, the best procedure is to turn it down in front of the player, then slide it into the side of the muck. Turning it down before taking it away gives the player warning that you're about to muck the hand. The first rule of poker is "Each player must protect his own hand," but if you grab the cards away too quickly the player may not even be aware you're about to muck them before they're gone. Also, if the player thinks you've misread the hand, you can still turn it back up before it reaches the muck to see who is right. (This, and the showing of a discarded hand at a player's request, are the *only* times that the dealer should turn up a player's cards.)

Dealers should never place an entire folded hand "on the muck." It should always be mixed into a non-stacked, "messy" muck.

In hold 'em or Omaha the high card of a flush is often on the board. It is meaningless to announce "King-high flush" if the king is on the board and two players have a flush (and neither has the ace). If there are three clubs on the board, and the player's cards are

it is better to announce "Flush with the queen," which would beat

(read as "Flush with the jack").

Announce a full house, for example, as "Treys full of kings"(3-3-3-K-K). In the case of two full houses, it is the three-of-a-kind that determines the winner. In hold 'em or Omaha it is possible for two or more players to each have a full house with the same three-of-a-kind, in which case the pair determines the winner. If the pair is also the same then they split the pot. The term "full of" designates a full house. Avoid slang terms such as "Full boat" or "No vacancy."

When reading hold 'em or Omaha hands, push the board cards forward for the best high hand you've seen so far. Push them forward only about one-half the length of the card; pushing them further may cause them to be confused with a player's cards. Keep the board neat.

Once a hand has been read and one or more board cards pushed forward, do not change the board cards unless you find a better high hand. When four board cards are being used it is acceptable to pull back the unused card instead of pushing forward the cards being used.

It is usually not necessary to push board cards forward when reading low hands, but if there is any confusion (typically due to counterfeited cards) then push forward the cards each player would use and call out all five cards one at a time starting at the high end. (Select the cards for low from bottom up, then read them from top down.)

Refer to the "Do's and "Don'ts" at the end of this book for more recommendations.

Showing a Discarded Hand

Often at showdown one player shows his hand, and others then discard theirs without showing them. Usually nothing else happens. Just muck the discarded hands and push the pot to the player with the live hand.

Sometimes, however, one of the other players will ask to see such a discarded hand. What you do at that point may depend upon house rules, but in most cases you should take the discarded hand, tap it on top of the muck to "kill" it, turn it face up for a few seconds for all players to see, then muck it.

In some rooms, only those other players who were also in the hand to the end have the right to ask to see a discarded hand. This is done because players who have just lost a large pot frequently find it irritating when they are forced to show their hand.[39]

Also, in some rooms, the hand is not killed before it is shown if it is the presumed winner who asks to see a discarded hand. In asking to see the hand, the presumed winner thus takes the risk that his opponent could turn out to be the winner. However, this is rarely done anymore.

---

[39]This rule is generally only enforced in high-limit games.

Hand Reading Exercises

Novice dealers frequently have trouble reading all hands correctly and quickly. Needless to say, awarding a pot to the wrong player will cause a dispute. Consequently, the following hand reading exercises are provided to get you "up to speed" in this area.

Reading Seven-Card Stud Hands

Shuffle the deck and deal out seven hands in the usual way (two down, four up, and one down). If you are doing this on a real poker table you should try for optimum positioning of players' cards on the table, giving you pitching practice at the same time.

Turn up one hand, bring the significant cards out front, and announce the value out loud. Then turn up the next hand, read it, and muck the lesser of the two (unless they tie). Continue until all hands have been read. This also gives you practice at mucking hands properly.

Reading Texas Hold 'em Hands

Deal out either nine or ten hands in the usual way (two down to each position). If you are doing this on a real poker table you should try for optimum positioning of the players' cards, giving you pitching practice at the same time. Put up the flop, turn, and river cards, including the burns, just as you would in a real game.

Turn up one hand, read it, push forward the appropriate board cards, and announce the value out loud. Then turn up the next hand, read it, change the board cards as appropriate, and muck the lesser of the two hands (unless they tie). Continue until all hands have been read. This also gives you practice at mucking hands properly.

Keep the board cards in two straight lines — the base line where they started and the front line of cards that are significant for the best hand read so far. The front line should be about one-half card length ahead of the base line; pushing them further forward may confuse them with players' hands that are across from the dealer. The front line should always be the significant cards for the best hand read so far.

Reading High-Low Split Omaha Eight-or-Better Hands

Deal out either nine or ten hands as for the hold 'em exercise above, except deal four cards to each position. Put up the board, and quickly analyze it. (See "Analyzing Omaha Eight-or-Better Boards" on page 125.)

Turn up one hand, *read it for high,* push forward the appropriate board cards, and announce the value out loud. Then turn up the next hand, read it, change the board cards as appropriate, and muck the lesser of the two hands unless they tie or unless the lesser hand may be in *contention for low.* Continue until all hands have been read for high.

Now go back and read all the hands for low (see "Reading Omaha Eight-or-Better Hands for Low" on page 128), again muck losing hands, except those that are winners for high.

Another Omaha Eight-or-Better Hand Reading Exercise

Shuffle a deck of cards and put up five board cards. Quickly analyze the board. Then put up four cards to represent a player's hand and read it against the board for *both high and low.*

Push the hand aside, put up the next four cards, and read that hand with the same board. Continue until most of the possibilities of the board have occurred, then shuffle and repeat.

Analyzing Omaha Eight-or-Better Boards

Omaha high-low split is generally considered to be the hardest poker game to deal. It is identical to Texas hold 'em with only two exceptions: Each player is initially dealt four cards instead of two, and final hands are read using exactly two hole cards with three board cards instead of simply the best five out of seven cards.

That doesn't sound too hard until you consider that there are six possible two-card combinations in each player's hand and ten possible three-card combinations of board cards, making a total of sixty possible five-card hands for each player.

Also, there are often five or more hands to read at showdown. This is because of the increased tendency of players to draw to either high or low, hoping that the other players are going the other way. These players have watched their hands develop through four rounds of betting, but they expect the dealer to read them all very quickly. The trick to reading Omaha eight-or-better hands is to know what you're looking for.

Take a few seconds to examine the board for key cards before attempting to read any player's hand. Suppose the board cards are

Let's consider the high possibilities first. The first step is to identify key cards, starting with the highest possible hands. Looking at this board, we see that no straight flush is possible, and there is no pair on the board so a full house or quads are likewise ruled out. However, a flush is possible. So do we go to the players' hands looking for a flush? Not quite so fast. Be specific. We are looking for two clubs! (Even if there were four or five clubs on the board, a player still needs two clubs in his hand to make a flush.)

In case no one has a flush, we note that a straight is also possible. So do we start looking at players' hands for a straight? Well, yes, but be specific in your mind about what you're looking for. In this case, there are two possible straights: ten-seven will make a jack-high straight, and queen-ten makes a queen-high straight. Note that either straight requires a ten, so the key card is a ten. If you find a ten, then look for either a seven or a queen to complete the straight.

If none of these hands exists, we must resort to looking for trips. Look for a pair in a player's hand, then check the board for a matching rank. Occasionally, it goes down to two pair or even one pair to win high (usually because everyone was playing for low).

Here is a copy of a chart used in the poker dealer class at Casino Gaming School as an exercise in reading an Omaha eight-or-better board:

Omaha Eight-or-Better Board Reading Exercise

For a straight, straight flush, or low, enter key card rank(s).
For a full house, enter rank of pair. For a flush enter suit.

Board Number:	1	2	3	4	5	6	7	8	9
Straight Flush / RF									
Full house / quads									
Flush									
Straight									
Low									
Straight/flush / RF									
Full house / quads									
Flush									
Straight									
Low									
Straight flush / RF									
Full house / quads									
Flush									
Straight									
Low									

Shuffle a deck of cards, then spread five cards to represent an Omaha board. Fill in column 1 for that board. Leave a category blank if such a hand is not possible. For the example board previously shown — J♣9♦8♣4♥2♣ the entries should be:

Straight Flush / RF: (blank)

Full House / Quads: (blank)

Flush: C (for clubs)

Straight: 10 (the key card for any straight)

Low: A,3 (the two lowest ranks not on the board)

You should use no more than ten seconds to analyze a board — five seconds is preferred — then pick up the cards, set them aside, and spread the next five cards off the deck. Now fill in column 2 for that board, and so on through the deck. As each board is picked up, stack it on top of the previous board cards. Fifty-two cards allow for ten boards, with two cards left over.

Now pick up the stack of cards and go through the same ten boards again, but much more slowly. You will probably notice that you have made several errors or omissions. As we said, reading hands in Omaha high-low split eight-or-better is not easy.

By the way, this exercise is not intended to be a test. The object of this exercise is to develop the ability to analyze a board quickly before reading the players' hands. With practice, you will pick up speed. Notice how little information is needed to be able to scan the players' hands for a winner. An experienced dealer should be able to fully analyze any board within five seconds.

Reading Omaha Eight-or-Better Hands for Low

First, confirm that there are at least three different rank cards eight or lower on the board (if not, then a low is impossible, and the high hand will take the entire pot). Again, tell yourself specifically what you are looking for before looking at players' hands.

It doesn't matter how high the board cards are so long as a low is possible. If there is no ace or deuce on the board then A-2 is a nut low whether the board's low cards are 3-4-5 (making a wheel that may also be in contention for high as a five-high straight) or 5-7-8, or any other combination of three different rank cards in the range three through eight.

Let's consider the same board as before; specifically:

In this case there are exactly three low cards on the board, so it is not possible to make a low with counterfeited cards. (A "counterfeited" card is any low card in a player's hand of the same rank as a board card.) Having exactly three low cards on the board makes it easy to compare low hands because:

a. To make a low, a player must have two cards of different ranks than any of the low board cards, and

b. Once such lows are found, it is only necessary to compare the players' cards without regard to the board cards.

The nut low is always the two lowest ranks that are not on the board (A-3 in this case). If you don't find that, look for A-5, and so on.

When there are four or five different rank low cards on the board it becomes possible to make a low with counterfeited cards. For example, suppose the board is:

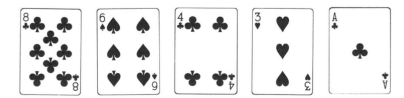

Since suit is not significant when reading low hands, we will not be concerned with suits for this board or for the players' hands. Now suppose the following five hands are in contention for low:

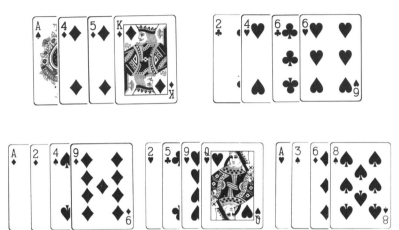

For ease of this example we have shown all of the cards in ascending order. This does not mean that you should organize the board and players' cards this way for reading.

When reading lows with counterfeited cards, it is necessary to select each player's best low from the bottom up, then read the hand from the top down. Let's do that for each of these five hands. Cards in outline are from the player's hand, and cards in normal type are from the board.

$$A\ 3\ 4\ 5\ 6 \quad A\ 2\ 3\ 4\ 6 \quad A\ 2\ 3\ 4\ 6$$

$$A\ 2\ 3\ 4\ 5 \quad A\ 3\ 4\ 6\ 8$$

In several cases we could have chosen board cards and player's cards differently, but the result would have been the same. In fact, all four cards in the fifth hand are counterfeited, yet it can make a low using any two from the hand and the three non-matching ranks from the board.

Now, reading these hands from the top down we find that the second and third hands are equivalent! Even though the players' hands are quite different, the effects of the counterfeited cards result in equal low hands.

Perhaps more surprising is that hand number four, which didn't look as good in the beginning, ended up making a wheel to win low. It is also the only hand to make a straight which will win high for a "scoop," unless someone else makes a flush. This occurs in hand number two, a flush with the 6♣2♣ for an eight-high club flush.

Another strange occurrence is a board such as:

Here we have four cards to a wheel on the board. What does it take for a player to make a wheel? Just a three won't do it because the player must use *two* cards from his hand and three board cards. In this case, a three plus any other "wheel card" will make a wheel.

Miscellaneous Procedures and Problem Handling

There are many minor (and some not so minor) problems that can come up during the play of a hand. Most of these can and should be handled by the dealer, but the dealer must know what circumstances require a floorperson's decision and act accordingly.

Unfortunately, many rules of poker are not universal. Consequently, the procedures and terminology described in this book and taught in any class are subject to change. You must be able to adapt to such differences wherever you work as a dealer. Here are a few problem situations and how they are usually handled:

Color Change

Sometimes a player will push out some chips and say "Color me up." This is a request to exchange his chips for higher denomination chips. Usually this should be done only between hands, and you should not annoy the other players by taking the time to accept chips that are not stacked. First, be sure you have room in the rack before agreeing to accept the chips. Then count down the chips, and give the player the same amount in larger chips before putting the player's checks in your bank. Since it's table stakes, all chips must still remain on the table unless the player is leaving the game. If they will not fit in your rack, offer the customer a chip rack or call a chiprunner. Do not hold up the game to "make them fit."

Oversize Chips

When there has been a bet and a player throws out an oversize chip with no announcement, the dealer should announce "Call."

That is a statement, not a question. If the player wants to raise, he must say "raise" *before* releasing the chip.

If there has been no previous bet for this round, the dealer should announce the size of the bet. (In a spread-limit game, don't assume the maximum bet; instead, ask the player how much he is betting.)

Unless you are able to follow the action while making change, just let the chip lay until the action is completed, then give the player his change as you are gathering the bets into the pot.[40]

If you do make change during the action, don't leave the oversize chip in front of the player. Instead, replace it with the correct amount of the bet or call as you bring the large chip into the pot.

Changing Up a Bill

Cash put in by a player for a bet is generally treated the same as an oversize chip. Of course this can occur only in a game where cash plays. In most cases, you should just announce the amount and continue to follow the action. Until you are quite experienced, you could lose control of the game if you stop to make change immediately.

When the action is complete, make change from the pot if possible. However, never leave cash in the pot in a low-limit game. Announce the amount being taken from the bill (e.g., "Eight out of twenty"). Measure off the bet first, then count down the remainder of the stack and announce the player's change (e.g., "Twelve change").

---

[40]It is usually best to make change from the pot in middle- and high-limit games whenever possible. This way the need for fills is kept to a minimum.

On the Piece Bets

A piece is currency (e.g., a $20 bill). So an "on the piece" bet is possible only in a game where cash plays. Also, some cardrooms may not allow on the piece bets even though cash plays, or it may be allowed only during the last betting round and/or only if the action is heads-up. Even so, any cash is generally changed up for chips, either immediately or at the end of the betting round, unless the player specifically says "On the piece." The rest of this section assumes that an on the piece bet has been requested by the player and that it is allowed in this particular circumstance.

A player wishing to bet or call who has cash on the table may push out a bill and say "Put it on the piece." The dealer will leave the bill in front of that player and place chips from the pot "on the piece" to mark the amount. Subsequent bets are added on the piece, but care must be taken that the amount marked is not allowed to exceed the value of the bill itself.

In the case of a later bet or raise, the dealer must ascertain the player's wish when the action reaches the player with the piece. If the player doesn't say anything, the dealer may simply ask "Call?" It is up to the player to say "raise" if that is his desire.

A player usually requests an on the piece bet because he hopes to win the pot and doesn't want the bill changed for chips. Therefore, if that player wins, the dealer should push the bill back to him along with the pot. However, if that player loses, the dealer should change up the bill from the pot (if possible) and give the player back his change before pushing the pot. (Alternatively, you can push the pot first and tell the winner how much more is coming from the piece).

If another player wins the pot, he may request that the bill be left in the pot. If this is permitted in your room, then give the player whose bet was on the piece his change from the pot, and push the piece along with the pot to the winner.

However, an exception occurs in low-limit games. Here you should change up "the piece" whenever possible. This will help insure that the player will stay in the game since he will still have chips to play with.

Foreign Chips

Often a player comes to the table with $1 blackjack or slot tokens or with chips from another casino. In the case of foreign chips, casinos are becoming much more sensitive to accepting them. In most poker rooms today they cannot be dropped into the drop box or placed in the rack. A chiprunner or floorperson should be called immediately for assistance in changing up these chips.

The metal $1 house tokens are very heavy and cause problems for security who collect the drop boxes. They do play, however, but should be changed up by the dealer and be given to the chiprunner along with the cash when getting a fill.

High denomination chip(s) also get special treatment. Follow the rules for your poker room. This usually includes calling a floorperson who will take the chip(s) to the main cage for conversion.

Counterfeit Chips

Casino chips are sometimes counterfeited (especially $100 chips). For this reason, house policy may change from time to time regarding certain foreign chi ps, and perhaps even the house's own large denomination chips. If you're not sure, ask the floorperson.

Straddle Bets

In hold 'em or Omaha, most cardrooms allow the first player after the big blind in hold 'em or Omaha to post a "straddle" before the cards are dealt. This is a blind bet, usually twice the size of the big blind, but in a spread-limit game it might be allowed to be anything from that up to the raise limit. When starting to deal the cards, announce "Live straddle...four to call" (or whatever the amount of the straddle). Since it is a live blind, that player has the last option to raise (assuming the cap has not been reached before it gets back to the straddle).

Soft Break

Often a player sits down in a small-limit game with a $100 bill. If he pushes out the bill and says nothing, go ahead and call for a rack of blue or change it with $80 in red chips and $20 in blue. If he objects or says he only wants to play a lesser amount, call out "Soft break," and ask the player how much he wants in chips. If no chiprunner is available, and you give him all chips, remind him that he may take any amount of chips (over the buy-in) off the table before he plays the first hand. (Do not hold up the game.) When the floorperson or chiprunner comes around, tell him how to break the bill; for example, "40/60 soft" means $40 in $1 chips and $60 in cash. The same procedure applies if a player has a black ($100) chip.

In some cardrooms, the dealer may "loan" the player a stack ($20) to play on until the chiprunner returns. If this is the case be sure the chiprunner hands the rack and cash to you and get the rack's $20 back before giving the balance to the player. There should be a $20 lammer in the bank to lay out while the bank is short. *Note: This is not a good practice, and for this reason it is generally not allowed in many cardrooms.*

Boxed Card

If a card is found to be face up in the deck during any part of the deal, it is called a "boxed card." Usually it is treated as a piece of paper (i.e., as if it's not even there). Announce it, let all the players see it, then put it face down in the muck. The next card immediately replaces it.

When Quarters Play

Obviously quarters play in a seven-card stud game when the bring-in is 50¢. In any game where quarters are being used for change (e.g., for the rake) they always play in increments of whole dollars. The question occurs when a player is going all-in and has less than $1 in quarters (besides any chips and multiples of four quarters). In some rooms the player is allowed to leave the odd quarters out or include them as part of the all-in bet as he chooses. However, if he goes all-in once, then goes all-in again in a later hand, the quarters must be omitted or included the same as the time before. (For this reason, in most poker rooms, quarters today only play in increments of one dollar.)

Folded Hand

If a player releases his cards face down with a forward motion, go ahead and muck it even if it might be in contention to win the pot. Exception: In a low-limit game you can push the hand back to the player in the big blind if there has been no raise or to a player who throws his cards in when there has been no bet. Generally, you extend this courtesy only once to each player.

Showing a Folded Hand

The policy of seeing a "called hand" or a "calling hand" that was discarded can be seen by any player at the table.[41] The dealer must tap the cards face down on the muck to "kill" the hand, then turn it face up on the table.

If a player abuses this privilege — that is, if he constantly asks to see other players' hands — he may be refused the right to see any hands. The floorperson will make this decision.

---

[41]If all players check this is still considered a called hand.

Show One, Show All

Most cardrooms have the policy that if a player shows a hand to one or more players at the table, any player can ask that the hand be shown. The dealer should then stop the hand before it is mucked. If the hand was shown to a player who still has a hand then the dealer should show it to the entire table immediately. Otherwise the cards should be set aside and shown when the hand is over.

Protecting the Pot

The primary aspect of protecting the pot is making sure that all bets are equal before pulling them into the pot and setting up a side pot if some player is all-in for less than the full bet. The dealer must also protect the pot from being "splashed" and *gently* inform a player who does splash the pot about the procedures, e.g., "Please place your bet in front of you so the other players can see how much you bet."

Making Change

Players may not make change for themselves from the pot. If a player reaches into the pot for change, ask him to "Please let the dealer make change for you." You may allow an exception to this if the player makes change only from his own previous bet of the current betting round that is still directly in front of him.

Uncorrectable Dealer Error

In most cases of dealer error, such as starting to deal the next round of cards before all action is completed, turning too many cards on the flop, turning the flop or other community cards before all the action is completed, giving a player too many cards, and the like, a floorperson must be called to make the decision. The dealer should never make such a decision on his or her own.

Correctable Dealer Error

In some cases of dealer error, such as forgetting to burn a card when dealing upcards, no one player is put at an advantage or disadvantage by the error, so the dealer may back up the cards without having to call a floorperson. However, if you are not sure, call the floorperson.

Checking for Enough Cards

When dealing seven-card stud, and there are still several active players after the sixth street betting round, check the stub of the deck to see if there are enough cards remaining to give each player a seventh card. Since you must burn a card, and the last card of the deck can never be used, you need at least two cards more than there are active players. If you don't have enough cards, call the floorperson.

The floorperson may tell you to burn and turn a community card face up in the middle of the table, which will act as each player's seventh card. Since stud players are not generally accustomed to community cards, the floorperson will usually stay to explain it to the players and see the hand through. The player who was high on sixth street is still first to act.

If shuffling the burns will make enough cards available, he may tell you to do that. Put the stub on the table, and do a small scramble to mix it with the burn cards; then cut onto the cut card as usual, burn a card, and deal a down card to each player.

Some cardrooms may have a different procedure, but these are the most common. The burn cards *are used* when the dealer fails to realize he doesn't have enough cards to complete the deal and some of the players have already received down cards. This is why clean burn cards are imperative.

One Player to a Hand

This has been mentioned before, and it's one of the cardinal rules of poker. Nevertheless, one aspect of this rule often eludes some dealers: Remember that neither another player, a friend sitting behind a player, *nor the dealer* may assist a player by turning the player's cards up; the player must do that himself. Do not attempt to read a hand until all of a player's cards are face up, and don't reach out and turn up a card that the player left face down. If the player is annoyed by this, simply inform him that you are not allowed to read a hand until the player turns up all his cards.

Check Out

In seven-card stud, if a player discards his hand when he could have just checked and if he does this before the burn, the seat takes no more cards. However, if it is a tie with the burn card the seat will take one more card. In some cardrooms, the seat takes cards until such time as there is a need for the hand to act.

Note: This latter policy often causes too much confusion and unnecessary errors. For this reason it is not recommended; however, check with your cardroom for their policy.

Misdeals

A misdeal is rarely called once significant action has taken place. In most cardrooms significant action is defined as two players who have acted on their hands — and this includes checking, betting, calling, or folding.

If significant action has not taken place, any of the following conditions generally cause a misdeal to be declared:

1. Failure to shuffle and cut the deck before dealing;
2. Dealing to the wrong player first;
3. Dealing too few or too many cards to one or more players;
4. The exposure of two or more cards that need to be replaced;
5. The presence of more than one boxed card;
6. The discovery of a duplicate or foreign card in the deck;[42]
7. The first card off the deck is exposed (or the second card in some rooms).

In the case of a misdeal, all the cards must be returned to the dealer to be reshuffled and redealt. Usually this does not require a floorperson's decision, but you should call a floorperson if any player objects.

---

[42]A duplicate or foreign card causes a misdeal regardless of the action. All players who started the hand are to receive their money back, and the hand is dealt again (with a different deck) with the same blinds and/or antes.

Taking the Rake

When first starting out, you should determine the rake and put it in the drop area immediately after each round of betting and before dealing the next round of cards, putting up the next board card, or calling for the showdown. This is part of the "accuracy before speed" policy.

When you have enough experience to be able to determine the rake quickly, even while you are doing other things, you should deal the next round or put up the next board card before getting the rake. Even when following this procedure, however, you must get the final rake before starting to read hands at showdown. It looks very bad to be taking money from the pot just as you are pushing it to the winner.

In any case, be as inconspicuous as possible about taking the rake. There's no need to call the players' attention to how much the house is taking out of the pot.

In most games the rake is either 5 percent or 10 percent as shown on the game placard, but higher stakes games may have a time collection instead. (See "Time Collection.") The following table will help you determine the rake quickly without having to multiply by a percentage.

Pot Size Steps		Amount of Rake
	5 Percent Rake	10 Percent Rake	

	5 Percent Rake	10 Percent Rake	Amount of Rake
Major Steps	$20.00	$10.00	$1.00
	$40.00	$20.00	$2.00
	$60.00	$30.00	$3.00
Minor Steps	$5.00	$2.50	1 quarter
	$10.00	$5.00	2 quarters
	$15.00	$7.50	3 quarters

First, determine the biggest major step in the amount in the pot. For example, suppose the rake is 5 percent and there is $49.75 in the pot. The biggest major step is $40.00, and the rake on that is shown to be two dollars. Next, consider the excess over that major step. There is only one step of $5.00 in the $9.75 remainder, for which the rake is one quarter.

It's easiest if you always think in terms of units, that is, chips and quarters rather than dollars and cents. In this example think of the rake as two chips and one quarter rather than as $2.25.

Never over-rake a pot (never round up). The above example's $49.75 pot must be raked for the lower step ($45.00), not for $50.00 even though the pot is only 25¢ short of that amount. For raking purposes, the amount already taken as rake is considered to still be part of the pot total, so any bets in the next betting round would be added to the $49.75 and the rake then made correct for the new total.

Many cardrooms now have posted on the table's placard what the rake schedule should be. For example, if the placard says "Take $1.00 on $40.00, $1.00 on $80.00, and $0.50 on $100" it means to rake one dollar after the pot reaches a total of $40, take another dollar after the pot reaches a total of $80, and to take a final fifty cents after the pot reaches a total of $100. In this example the maximum rake would be $2.50.

Side Pot Rake

Nevada gaming regulations state only that the maximum rake is 10 percent of "all monies wagered." Nothing is said about side pots, so the key word seems to be "all." Therefore, it appears to be technically correct to rake from the currently active side pot to make the rake correct for the total of all pots up to the legal limit.

The rake is taken by percentage from each pot as it is reached. For example, if there is $20 in the main pot, $15 in the first side pot, and $8 in the second side pot, and the rake is 10 percent to $4.00 maximum, you should rake $2.00 from the main pot, $1.50 from the first side pot, and $0.50 from the second side pot. This assures "fairness of rake" among all the players, since the total rake is not taken from the main pot. (Never go back and rake more from a previous pot, as you would then be over-raking that pot.)

Often it is best to defer raking a small side pot. For example, suppose the rake is 5 percent, and there is $19.00 in the main pot and $2.00 in a side pot. You rake three quarters from the main pot, then you realize that the side pot brings the total to $21.00, and a quarter should be raked from the side pot to bring the rake to the correct $1.00 total. However, it would look bad to the players to rake a quarter from such a small pot. It's better to defer the rake until the side pot grows on the next betting round (but remember that you started with $21.00). The worst that can happen is that there is no more betting, and you end up pushing the side pot without raking it. Most cardrooms will not object if you occasionally under-rake by one quarter due to these circumstances. Under-raking is always preferable to over-raking, but you should always try to get as close to the proper percentage as possible without going over.

Rake in Other Jurisdictions

California and some other jurisdictions do not allow the rake to be related to the pot size. For this reason, a fixed per-hand fee is taken from the antes or blinds and is dropped before the cards are even dealt. It would seem that the fixed per-hand fee would take up a large portion of the initial pot; however, these games usually start with more money in the pot due to the fact that they have a higher ante structure than most small-limit games that are raked.

In other places the cardroom may take a one-step or two-step rake. (e.g, $1 on $40 and $1 on $80). In this case, there is no rake until the pot reaches the specified amount, but once the pot reaches that amount, the rake is taken. In some cases, additional rake is taken when the pot reaches another (higher) specified amount. Unlike the fixed per-hand fee, which is dropped before the cards are dealt, the rake is dropped *after* the hand is completed.

Time Collection

A time collection is used in most high-stakes games and in all games in some jurisdictions. In such games there is no per-hand rake or drop. Instead, the house collects a per-player fee on a time basis, typically every half hour. There are two common ways this is done: by direct collection from each player, or by indirect collection from the pot — known as a "time pot."

The dealer usually takes the time immediately after he or she arrives at the table. This is done by announcing "Time" or "Time pot."

More common in the higher stakes games is indirect collection from the pot. In this case, it is the dealer's responsibility to collect the time. The dealer, while shuffling the first hand, will announce "Time pot."

In games where the time is collected from the antes and the time charge is *small* compared to the total of the antes, the dealer will take the time for the number of players at the table from the pot. This is done after the antes are brought into the center, and that total revenue is placed on the drop slot. For example, in an eight-handed $75-$150 stud game with a $15 ante and a $5 time charge, the dealer will take $40 from the initial pot and place it on the drop slot. In games where the time is collected from the antes and the time charge is *large* compared to the total of the antes, the players will double ante. The dealer will then take the time for the number of players at the table from the pot. This is done after the *double* antes are brought into the center, and the total revenue is placed on the drop slot. For example, in an eight-handed $30-$60 stud game with a $5 ante and a $4 time charge, the dealer will take $32 from an initial $80 in antes, rather than the usual $40 in antes. This is done so that the pot is still worth playing for. In both cases, on approval by the floorperson, the dealer drops the collection.

If there is a seat with chips but the player is absent, the fee is taken from the player's stack of chips, and brought in with the antes. Any person that is "playing over" is also required to pay time, however, their money remains in the pot since the house cannot collect more money than it has seats. Depending on house policy, a new player may not be required to pay the fee if five minutes or more have passed before he gets a seat or if there is no one waiting for the game.

Time pots in flop games are taken as follows. The dealer upon shuffling for the first hand announces "Time pot." The time in these games is generally taken after the flop — the first hand with a flop is where the time is taken. Multiply the number of active players (including any player who is away from the table, since their time has been taken from their stack and placed into the pot) and take the total revenue and place it on the drop slot. (Any person who is playing over must pay also, but again their money stays in the pot.)

In hold 'em games, when time is collected per player, you should start collecting "time" from the one seat and continue around the table to the last seat, making change where necessary, placing the revenue on the drop slot. In stud games, when time is collected per player, you should start collecting the "time" and antes from the one seat and continue around the table to the last seat, making change where necessary. Leave the total amount of the antes in the center of the table and place the revenue on the drop slot. A floorperson will record the time and instruct you to drop it.

In very high-limit games with blinds, the time is taken directly from the small blind before the cards are dealt. In these games you do not wait for a flop. In addition, time is typically taken every fifteen or twenty minutes depending on the number of players.

Jackpot Rake

Some cardrooms have a "Bad Beat" jackpot, which is won by the players when a very strong hand loses to an even stronger hand in their jackpot games.[43] See the chapter on "Jackpots" for information about how they work. What we are concerned with here is not the jackpot itself but the separate and additional rake taken to build the jackpot.[44]

Typically, either a predetermined amount of the ante is dropped for the jackpot, or the jackpot rake is taken on a percentage basis. The jackpot rake is placed in a separate position on the table, and it is dropped in its own separate box or other container at the same time the regular rake is dropped.

Since there is much variation between rooms regarding how much is raked for the jackpot, we won't go into detail here. Ask your shift manager about this.

---

[43]The players who win the Bad Beat jackpot will vary depending on the poker room. In some rooms only the holders of the winning and losing hands will share in the prize. In other rooms all players at the table will share in the prize.

[44]A few cardrooms will offer these jackpots without any additional rake.

Side Pot Procedures

A side pot occurs as a result of the table stakes rule when any player wants to bet or call but doesn't have enough money on the table.

In some cases a second and even a third player may go all-in during the same hand (especially during tournament play). The dealer must start a new side pot each time another player goes all-in for a different amount. Here are the procedures for creating side pots:

One Short Bet (or Two of the Same Size)

1. Multiply the amount of the all-in bet times the number of active players (including the all-in player). Put this amount into the main pot (or currently active side pot), and rake from that pot to make the rake correct for the new total of all pots up to that point.
2. Gather the remaining bets together to form the new side pot, and rake from that pot to make the rake correct for the total of all pots. (In some rooms, the policy is to rake the side pot based on just the amount in each pot. This often takes a little less than the maximum permitted rake, but it avoids the appearance of over-raking.)

Two (or More) Short Bets of Different Sizes

1. Start with the smallest bet. Bring it toward the center of the table, then go clockwise around the table pulling in an equal amount from each bet until you return to where you started (as evidenced by a bet pulled out with no money behind it). Put

these partial bets into the currently active pot, and rake that pot.

2. Repeat step 1, starting with the smallest remaining bet, to form a new side pot. Rake each pot as it is formed.

3. Continue repeating as often as necessary. When all remaining bets are equal, they are gathered together to become the last side pot.

If the player who went all-in seems confused, then as the side pot is formed you can tell him that he is in for the main pot, and that the other players will continue betting on the side.

At the end of all action, the winner of each pot must be determined in the reverse order in which the pots were formed. It may be helpful to use chips or coins to set a pointer from the current pot to the player who went all-in and caused the new side pot to be created. The last side pot will not have a pointer because to decide it you want to see all hands that *do not* have a pointer to them. Then, as you go back through the side pots, each pointer tells you which hand you want to see next.

(Note: The maximum number of side pots is two less than the number of players remaining in the hand since there must be at least two players in the main pot.)

Stub Counts

The stub (remainder of the deck) is periodically counted to assure that the deck contains the proper number of cards. The purpose is to assure the integrity of the deck.

In General

1. After the last card has been dealt, count the remaining cards into a separate pile, in front of the rack but not mixed with the muck or burn cards. Continue to follow the table action while you're counting. If you must make an announcement, restack bets, make change, or do something else to keep the action going, you should pause on a number you can easily remember, then resume the count when you again have both hands available.

2. Do not delay the game to complete the stub count. If all action is completed and the players are ready for the showdown before your stub count is completed you should abandon the stub count and immediately start reading the hands.

3. Most rooms stipulate that the *stub count must be completed at least once per down* and more frequently as time permits. If it's getting close to the end of your down and you haven't yet completed a stub count, *you must finish a count* even if it delays the game. If necessary, you can put the remainder of the stub down beside the rack while you read hands and push the pot, then pick it back up and complete your count.

4. If the stub count is incorrect, you should change the deck. Discreetly inform the next dealer and the floorperson when you're pushed.

Seven-Card Stud

1. The stub and muck must be combined. Gather the muck together into a small pile, leaving the burn cards where they are. Slide the stub (with its cut card still on the bottom) under the muck, and square up the pile — face down on the table — on top of the cut card.
2. Pick up the squared up stack with the cut card still on the bottom. Count to seven, then repeat, beginning each count at one. The last count should end on six.[45]
3. Do not attempt a stub count if you had to shuffle the burns or put up a community card.

Hold 'em

1. If all players are present in a ten-handed game, there should be twenty-four cards in the stub. (The muck is not combined with the stub.)
2. If there were fewer players, add two for each seat that was not dealt a hand. If there were more than ten players, subtract two for each additional player who was dealt a hand.

---

[45]For those of you mathematically inclined here's why this procedure works. There are four burn cards and n players will take all seven cards (to the river). Thus the the number of cards contained in the stub plus the muck will be

$$52 - 4 - (7)(n) =$$
$$48 - 7n =$$
$$(6)(7) + 6 - 7n =$$
$$(6 - n)(7) + 6$$

Consequently when dividing the number of cards left in the muck by 7 there will always be a remainder of 6.

Omaha

1. The stub count will always be a multiple of four.

High Draw and Lowball Draw

1. Figure the total of the burn card and all draws in your head. For example, if the draws were 2, 1, 3, pat, 2, this totals 9 (including the burn card).
2. Multiply the number of players who were dealt starting hands by 5, and add this to the total of the draws.
3. Start your stub count with the next number. For example, if seven players were dealt starting hands, and the draws were as in No. 1 above, you figure 7 x 5 + 9 = 44, so you start the stub count at 45. The count should end at 52 (53 if there's a joker in the deck).

Floorperson's Decision

Never challenge a floorperson's decision at the table. If you disagree with the decision, an option may be to say something like "I think there might be a misunderstanding. May I repeat the situation?"

If you are still confused, you should talk to the floorperson at the earliest opportunity, and ask "When *[describe the situation]* occurred, why did you rule *[as you did]?*" Open discussions between management and cardroom staff are generally welcome at the appropriate time and in the proper place.

Regarding decisions: The dealer is responsible for imparting the facts concerning the immediate problem only. Impressions and opinions are both unnecessary and destructive to the decision-making process. Further, when calling for a decision always call out your table number. Example: "Decision, table number 27."

Dealer Lineup

In most cardrooms, each dealer is in the box for twenty or thirty minutes before being pushed by the next dealer. Your time in the box is called a "down," and the sequence of dealers going through the line of games is the "dealer lineup." The procedure for pushing the line is generally as follows:

When tapped by the next dealer, you should:

1. Complete the current hand, including all final actions.[46]
2. Square up the deck, cross the deck, and place it a few inches in front of the bank. Place the cut card in front of the cards.
3. Push your chair back and stand up. Clap your hands lightly, and show your hands palms up.
4. If you were tapped on your left shoulder, you should get up to your right, and vice versa. Stand up, but don't turn your back on the table; be sure the next dealer is actually there and ready to sit down before you leave the table. *Never leave the rack unguarded.*

---

[46]Never argue over whether you are being taken out of that particular game too early or too late. If you feel you have been treated unfairly, talk to the floorperson. Never refuse to get up when tapped. (An exception may be if you just sat down and you think the other dealer has the lineup wrong, or if you dealt a jackpot hand which hasn't yet been paid off. See "Jackpot Procedures" for more information.)

5. Check the lineup to determine where you go next.[47] Don't delay between tables; you will be cutting short the break of the last dealer in the line, and you wouldn't want that to happen to you.

6. You may want to move the tokes from your shirt pocket to a trouser pocket or handbag as you are walking to the next table.

7. If going to another table, gently tap that dealer on the shoulder and wait quietly until he or she gets up. Don't change sides after tapping the dealer, or he will be getting up directly in front of you, making it difficult to exchange places. While waiting, check the placard for information about the game and rake, and start eyeballing the rack for a preliminary count.

8. Once seated, toss an absent button to the stack of chips of any player not at the table. An accumulation of three absent buttons indicates that the player has been gone over an hour, and the floorperson should be informed.[48] If there is a waiting list, the floorperson may pick up the player's checks and allow a new player to enter the game.

9. *Get the game going again quickly!* Don't make the players wait any longer than necessary for the dealer change.

10. Continue counting the bank while shuffling. By the time the first hand is completed, you should know how much cash should be in the well, and you can complete the count very

---

[47]The lineup may be standard for the room, with any variations given verbally by the floorperson, but more often there is a lineup or break table board displayed at the podium. The shift manager will explain how the list works.

[48]This is in rooms that use twenty-minute downs. Some rooms use thirty-minute downs. When this is the case an absent player is usually allowed two buttons plus fifteen minutes before it is necessary to inform the floorperson.

quickly. Report any shortage to the floorperson immediately. If the rack is short and you wait too long before reporting it, you may become responsible for the shortage.[49] [50]

11. If going on break, there may be things to do such as brushing the room (cleaning ashtrays, picking up trash and empty glasses, etc.). Always let the floorperson know if you are leaving the room (e.g., to go to the restroom or to cash in the change in your pocket).

12. Some casinos allow dealers to play the slots or video poker while on break. If you want to do this, ask the floorperson for permission, be sure he/she knows where you will be, and get back in time to push the line. Don't play right up to the last minute; you might be delayed by a hand pay jackpot or hopper fill.

13. After your break, be sure to report to your assigned table at the appointed time. This is known as pushing the line. If the lineup has changed, tell the dealer you're pushing about the changes.

---

[49]Most cardrooms allow five minutes from the time you sit down to count the bank. This gives you time to deal one hand rather than stalling the action while you count the bank. If you report a shortage within the allotted time, you will not be responsible for it. Also, some cardrooms allow shortages up to a specified threshold to go unreported, but be sure you know what that threshold is before you forego reporting a shortage.

[50]If you are in a cardroom where you carry your own bank this step is not necessary.

Jackpot Procedures

Many cardrooms feature a "Bad Beat Jackpot." This jackpot is won when a very strong hand (of a specified minimum value) loses to an even stronger hand. Various conditions of the jackpot, such as "Both hole cards must play and must make up that player's best five-card hand," will be posted in the room or in a brochure.

In nearly all jackpot games, a specific additional and separate rake is taken from each pot and placed into the jackpot drop. (See "Jackpot Rake on page 148.") This revenue goes into the jackpot pool, which is separate from all other monies in the casino and is kept in a separate jackpot account. This money "belongs to the players." Most cardrooms featuring jackpots take a fixed percentage administrative fee to cover the cost of security, the count room, cashiering, special tournaments for the jackpot players only, and other functions of the administration of the jackpot pool.

When it appears that the jackpot conditions have been met by the hands shown, the dealer will immediately call the floorperson to verify the fact. Once it has been verified, the floorperson will instruct the dealer to "run down" the deck. The dealer will gather all cards that are not actually involved in making up the jackpot hands, separate them by suit, and sort each suit so that the floorperson can easily verify that the deck in play is in compliance with a standard deck. Should there be a deviation (i.e., a card missing, two cards of the same rank and suit, extra cards, etc.) the jackpot will most likely be declared null and void. (This is another good reason to do stub counts regularly.)

Depending on house rules, any conversation during the play of a hand indicating that one player already has a jackpot hand or is drawing to a jackpot hand, or remarks that lead other players to believe that this is the time to attempt to play for a jackpot, may render any subsequent jackpot null and void. We consider this a questionable rule because any such decision would necessarily be very subjective.

Only the two best hands will qualify for the jackpot award, except where two hands are of equal value and therefore split their part of the jackpot. For example, if there are four sevens, four jacks, and a straight flush, only the straight flush and the four jacks qualify for the jackpot.

The dealer just sits in the box, watching the table, until the floorperson indicates that the cards may be gathered and the game resumed. If it comes time to push, the other dealers typically just bypass that table in the lineup until the next push comes after the jackpot has been paid off. This is because the dealer who dealt the jackpot hand can expect some very good tokes, but many of the players are likely to "forget" about toking if that dealer is gone from the table.

In most cardrooms, the jackpot is divided up something like this: The winning hand gets 25 percent of the jackpot, the "bad beat" hand (best losing hand) gets 50 percent, and the remaining 25 percent is divided equally among the other players at the table who were dealt in to the hand. In some rooms part of the jackpot money may even be split among players at other tables.

Depending on house policy, an employee who is playing while "on the clock" (e.g., a prop, shill, dealer, or floorperson) may not be eligible to win the jackpot. If that person is involved in a jackpot situation then the proper portions of the jackpot are awarded to the other players, but the employee's portion stays in the jackpot pool.

When anyone who is ineligible to collect the jackpot wins a pot, the jackpot rake is returned to the pot before the pot is pushed since it would not be fair to collect a jackpot fee in that case.

Dealing a Tournament

There are many differences between dealing live games and tournaments. We will try to cover most of them here.

Prize Pool and House Fee

There is no rake or time collection during tournament play. Instead, the buy-in consists of two parts: the portion that goes into the prize pool, and an entry fee that goes to the house. Most of the buy-in generally goes into the prize pool. Sometimes the buy-in and entry fee are stated separately so that the players will know exactly how much is going into the prize pool. Typically, all rebuy money goes into the prize pool.

Rebuys

Small tournaments often have a rebuy period, such as the first hour of play. In some cases, the dealer sells the rebuy; in others the floorperson must be called. In most cases, a player may rebuy any time he has less than the starting amount of chips. Rebuys usually cost the same as the original buyin less the entry fee. In some cases the rebuys are progressive. That is, the amount of tournament chips received for a rebuy goes up roughly in proportion to the stakes at the time.[51] At the end of the rebuy period there may be an optional double rebuy or "add on." That is, a player may have the option to purchase twice the amount in tournament chips for the same price as earlier rebuys regardless of how much he has in tournament chips at the time. It is important to note that dealers should always shuffle *before* issuing

---

[51]Sometimes these progressive rebuys cost more as the tournament goes on.

rebuys. This is to insure that the hands with rebuy delays may still be played at that limit.

Deal to All Players

The most obvious difference to the dealer is that cards are dealt to all seats where there are player's chips *regardless of whether or not there is a player in the seat.* All antes, blinds, and/or bring-in bets must be paid; if a player isn't there, the dealer or another player puts in the chips from the missing player's stack. A hand dealt to an empty seat remains live until there is a bet, then it is folded. However, if the player returns before the hand is folded, he may play it. Since every player is dealt in every hand, there is no need for missed blind buttons. There will be a dead small blind only if a player is knocked out of the tournament in the hand where he paid the big blind.

Tokes in a Tournament

Although poker dealers generally don't pool their tokes, a toke pool is the only practical way to handle tokes in a tournament. No one tokes the dealer during tournament play. (It wouldn't be any good even if they did as the chips have no cash value.) Instead, the winners (generally) toke part of their prize money at the end. In some cases, part of the buy-in (or part of an optional add-on) goes into the dealers' toke pool.

The tokes are typically divided among the dealers as follows: Each time you sit down to deal a table, you sign your name on a slip of paper in the rack, thus recording that you dealt one down. At the end, the tournament manager accumulates the number of names on each slip to determine the total number of downs. That number is divided into the total tokes to determine the per-down toke. The number of downs is determined for each dealer and multiplied by the per-down toke to determine the amount due each dealer.

Part
5
Miscellaneous

Miscellaneous

Introduction

Even though we have covered a great deal of material so far in this text, there are still a few additional topics that we need to address. These include maintaining dealer integrity, controlling the game, getting started as a dealer, and how to land a dealing job.

We will also mention some "do's and don'ts." Please read them carefully and when in the box do your best to abide by them.

Maintaining Game Integrity

Sometimes you will be dealing and a player will lose several hands in a row. Frequently he won't blame himself for the losses, and he doesn't want to attribute it to bad luck, so someone must take the blame. If he's an inexperienced player, he might even think he's been cheated.[52]

Often these frustrated players will blame the dealer. You are the only one handling the deck, shuffling, and so forth, so you may become the target. You cannot avoid this situation, but you should always be careful to maintain proper dealing procedures. Specifically:

The Muck

Don't massage the muck or square it up; leave it "messy." Never put a folded hand on the top or bottom of the muck. Always mix folded hands into the muck. The stub should be dropped in a short slide on top of the muck so that the top of the deck is retrievable in case there is any irregularity on the deal. The winning hand should never be placed on top of the muck; just turn it down and start your scramble. (In flop games the board cards are also treated this way.) Also, when the hand is over, break up any trips, quads, or other strong holdings.

---

[52]In our experience cheating is very rare in public cardrooms. One reason for this is that public cardrooms are well aware that cheating is bad for business and are thus very diligent about keeping their games clean. Another reason is that the players themselves tend to be on the lookout for suspicious activities and are usually quick to report any concerns they may have to cardroom management.

The Deck

Always do a good scramble. It only takes a couple seconds if you spread the cards out over the available space. Do an especially good scramble any time the deck is changed, regardless of whether it's a setup or a used deck from the well.

Always start and end the shuffle sequence with a riffle, never a box, and never box twice in a row.

Square up the deck before cutting. A suspicious player may think that an offset is intentional so you can cut there.

Place the deck in your hand immediately after the cut. You should always hold onto the deck while a hand is in progress, but if it becomes necessary to put the deck down before a hand is finished, place it on the table in front of the rack, and place a chip or button on top of the deck. Then pick up the deck and place it in your hand removing the cover chip.

Keep the deck level or pointed slightly down at all times. Yes, the bottom of the deck is covered so the players can't see the bottom card, but that's not the point. This will minimize flashed cards and insure that everyone's "down cards" are private.

Never pull a card off the deck. Always push the top card over with the thumb of the hand holding the deck and grasp it at the front corner. This is to avoid suspicion that you might be dealing "seconds."

Never cover the deck with your other hand. This is to avoid suspicion that you might be placing a palmed card on top of the deck. If you must square up the deck, place the index finger of your hand in front of the deck and tap on the back end with your right knuckle.

Never put a card back on the deck unless it was an extra card off the deck, and make sure the players understand why you are putting it back. If a card accidentally went to the wrong seat, just slide it to the right seat.

The Pot

It is your responsibility to protect the pot. This includes, but is not limited to the following:

1. Bring in all bets before dealing the next card or reading hands. Failure to do so may make a player think that the chips in front of him are actually change and he might return them to his stack.[53]

2. Be sure all bets are equal before bringing them in. A very common dealer error is bringing in the bets before the action is complete or change needs to be made.

3. Be ready at all times to prevent a player from splashing the pot. If a player does splash the pot, place the bet back in front of the player and say "Please don't splash the pot." However, if that same player does it again, you should assume that he didn't understand. This time, say "Please place your bet directly in front of you so the other players can see how much you bet." Be ready to interpose with your hand the next time it is that player's turn to act.

4. Don't handle the pot unnecessarily. Don't gather it into a small pile until preparing to push it to the winner. (A pot that is spread out looks bigger and contributes to the feel of an "action" game.)

5. If there's an all-in player, make the side pot clear to the players.

6. Get the final rake before reading hands. You don't want to be taking a rake as you are pushing the pot.

7. Keep the pot away from the rack. If chips fall from the pot into the rack you may have to count the rack and/or the pot to be sure it's correct.

---

[53]The exception would be a split-pot game with only two players remaining in the hand. Now any bets should remain in front of the players until the outcome of the hand is determined.

8. Don't splash the pot when making change. Just as the players have a right to see that each player is putting the correct bet into the pot, they should not have to wonder if you are making change correctly.

9. If you make a color change, do it in front of the rack, and be sure it is clear what you are doing, without delaying the game.

10. When pushing the pot, don't sweep too close to the other players' chips. Move the board cards, and so forth, out of the way, and push the pot down the center of the table and directly to the winner.

Controlling the Game

As the dealer, it is your responsibility to control the game and run it in a quiet and efficient manner. Here are some guidelines.

1. Use clear and concise language to control the game. You must talk enough to keep the action going and to keep all players informed, but don't overdo it.

2. Use "sir" and "ma'am" sparingly. These terms are important, but they may begin to lose their value if overused. Use them primarily when thanking a player for a toke or to get a player's attention. (For example, you can say "Thank you, sir," or "Two to you, ma'am.")

3. Some women don't like to be addressed as "ma'am," perhaps feeling that it implies age more than respect; use "miss" instead. First names are common at the poker table, so it's okay to use her first name if she gives it to you.

4. The word "please" can never be overworked. Use it frequently, as in "Blinds please," "Please don't splash the pot," and "Please act in turn."

5. Always thank a player immediately for a toke. Try to make eye contact, as this adds sincerity to the thanks. Show gratitude in your voice, but always do it the same regardless of the size of the toke. Don't fawn over a player because of an unusually large toke, and don't sound disgruntled because of a small toke or none at all. Remember to tap the edge of the rack lightly before putting the toke in your pocket.

6. Never tell a player he *must* do something. The player always has options. For example, suppose a player bets $3, and the next player puts in $5. Don't say "You have to make it six." Instead, just push back the extra chips and say "The bet was only $3." If the player says "I'm raising two" you can then explain "I'm sorry, but a raise must be at least equal to the bet." If his attempted raise was at least half the bet (as it was in this example), then he may still raise $3 if he wishes. Always

inform the player of his options rather than telling him he "has to" do a specific thing.[54]

7. Be courteous to all customers at all times, even if they are not courteous themselves. The other players will appreciate your self-control.

8. Never make a comment about to how a customer played a hand or express an opinion of how a hand should have been played.

9. Give the game you are dealing your undivided attention. It is your responsibility to run the game, and you can't do it if your mind is elsewhere. Stay completely focused and alert while you are in the box.

10. Never use slang or derogatory terms to describe hands, to get a player's attention, to announce the action, or in reference to a player or a player's actions.

11. Maintain a presence about yourself when in the box. Sit upright, do not slouch, display interest in the game and the players.

12. Always make your movements quickly, smoothly, and efficiently, demonstrating your professionalism. Never try to "fancy up" your moves or actions, such as a high, spinning "helicopter" pitch of the last player's upcard. To most players it is only a sign of nonprofessionalism. You may impress a tourist, but you'll only annoy the regular players who are more interested in an error-free, fast-paced game than in showmanship.

13. Never argue with a customer or get involved in an argument between players. In case of any disagreement, call a floorperson. After making a decision, the floorperson leaves the table, and annoyance can dissipate. You do not have the option to leave the table, so stay neutral and proceed with your job.

---

[54]If a player continues to make these "unannounced" raises the floorperson may rule that any future raise of this type will not stand.

14. Never imply through the tone of your voice, your actions, or your mannerisms that the customer is anything less than the most valuable asset the casino has.
15. Point with your eyes, not your finger. If you say "It's up to you," most players will look at your face to see who you're talking to. Also, don't pat the table in front of a player to get his attention unless it's absolutely necessary, as this can be taken as condescending. Should the need arise, use an open hand with a polite "It's on you, sir."
16. Never rush or attempt to deal so fast that you compromise technical or procedural requirements. Remember: "Accuracy before speed."
17. Project a positive attitude about your job and your fellow employees.
18. Excessive conversation is not good public relations. You are expected to be polite, but you should never initiate a conversation or extend a conversation at the table. If a player wants to converse with you, you should give a short, polite answer, but proceed with dealing. There is never any reason for nonbusinesslike conversations with anyone not seated at your table.
19. Don't be sympathetic over a player's loss or jubilant over a player's win. Remember, for every winner there is always a loser.
20. It can go without saying that dealers have a natural resentment toward a "stiff" (non-toker). However, such a player should be treated as well as any other. Even the non-tokers are important to your income because without them there might not be a game for you to deal. Also, the subject of tokes should never be discussed within earshot of any player.

Examples of
Bad Player Etiquette

Dealers are not the only ones who are sometimes guilty of bad etiquette. Even though player behavior is not the thrust of this book, we mention it so that you will know what to recognize in order to call a floorperson. Remember, even if a player behaves poorly, it is not your job to discipline him. Here are some examples of annoying conduct on the part of a player.

1. Bending or breaking cards
2. Not showing down a winning hand in proper order when the action is over
3. Throwing cards
4. Boisterous behavior that annoys other players
5. Splashing chips into the pot, making it hard for others to count them
6. Making any actions that are ambiguous or unclear
7. Waiting unnecessarily long to see if a player behind will reveal his intentions
8. Criticizing another player for the way he played his hand
9. Showing impatience with beginners
10. Refusing to show a called hand when asked by another player
11. Deliberately acting out of turn
12. Improper language or gestures
13. Speaking any language other than English during the play of a hand
14. Concealing one's cards (when playing hold 'em, Omaha, and other board games)
15. Deliberately overstating a hand
16. Blowing smoke at others.

The floorperson should be called if a player repeatedly commits any of these offenses or if one player complains about another. Again, it is not your job to discipline offending players.

Assuring the
Integrity of the Games

A poker room not only has to *have* a high level of integrity, it also must have the perception of integrity. That is, not only should a cardroom's games be "squeaky clean," but its patrons need to know that this is the case. Otherwise it is our experience that customers will find another place to play.

If you suspect any type of devious behavior at your table, or in your cardroom, you should not do anything at the table to show your suspicions. Instead, you should discreetly inform the floorperson after you leave the table. You might also tell the next dealer when you're pushed.[55]

Fortunately, cheating in cardrooms is extremely rare. However, here are a few things to watch out for:

Collusion

The number one fear of poker players, especially inexperienced ones, is that two or more players will be colluding against them. An example of collusion would be when one "partner" has a powerful hand, he signals his confederate, and they raise each other back and forth to the limit to get the maximum money in the pot from other players who may be unaware of what is going on. At the end, the one with the weak hand simply mucks his cards, so that you don't see that he was raising with nothing.

This is one reason for the rule allowing anyone at the table to see a called hand. An alert team player will counter by discarding

---

[55]Some cardrooms have procedures such as asking for a new setup and saying that the cards are "sticky" to alert the floorperson of a possible problem.

without calling the strong hand's last raise so that no one can ask to see his hand.

It is our experience that collusion today is very rare. When it does occur it usually shows itself in a small-limit game with two very amateurish players as partners. In most games the players themselves act as "the police," and this type of problem does not emerge. Should you suspect this type of problem, inform your floorperson discretely so they can take appropriate action.

Holding out Cards

Another form of cheating is holding out cards. For example, a player might be dealt an ace and a useless second card. He hides the ace and throws the other card directly into the muck; he may even act out of turn so he can throw it into the muck when the dealer isn't watching. In a later hand he switches the held out ace for an unneeded card.

The primary reason that you do a stub count is to detect and deter holdouts. Counting the stub is the most effective countermeasure to use against hold-out specialists, since just seeing the dealer count the stub warns them that it is likely they will be detected. Be sure to complete a stub count at least once per down, and at other times whenever time permits.

It is very important when changing setups that the new deck you put in play is the opposite color from the previous deck. This will also deter a "hold-out artist" for obvious reasons.

Marking Cards

Another thing to watch for are marked cards. The most common way of marking plastic cards is to put a tiny crease in the edge of the card, usually the end so it can be seen in the deck in the dealer's hand. The position of the crease may indicate the rank of the card. Such a card should be taken out of play, and you should watch for any player intentionally creasing cards.

If you work in a casino where the players are allowed to eat at the table, watch for food stains. Mustard is especially useful for marking cards, and it looks accidental since the player is eating — even an accidental stain can be utilized by an alert player. If you can't remove the stain, the deck should be taken out of play.

Toking "In House"

The "brush toke" is a tradition used to thank brushpcople, chiprunners, desk clerks, and/or card handlers for keeping our cardrooms, and more particularly our games running smoothly and efficiently. New players are introduced to the cardroom, empty seats are kept clean and filled, the rack is kept full so players won't have to wait to get in action — these are just a few of the ways the staff members support dealers. Furthermore, without those staff members dealers would once again be spending their breaks doing these jobs.

Usually the brush toke is paid after completing at least two hours of your shift — though this may vary between cardrooms. While not mandatory this toke is important. Please realize the value of the services provided by the staff. Always keep in mind that these people allow you, the dealer, to earn more money and utilize your break time any way you choose.

Getting Started

Getting a job as a poker dealer may require some leg work. The three things that you will probably need to do are:

1. Fill out a job application (and possibly have an interview) in the Personnel department (also known as "Human Resources");
2. Pass an audition; and
3. Get a gaming card.

If you are being sent for an audition by a school or employment agency, all you need to do initially is what is described under "Going for an Audition" on page 182. However, there is no reason why you can't try for a job on your own. First, talk to the cardroom manager. A telephone call is *not* recommended. Make sure you are well dressed (preferably in "black and whites," in case of an on the spot audition), go to the cardroom where you would like to work, and ask to see the manager on duty. If the cardroom manager is not there, ask when would be a good time to return. Make an appointment if possible.

When you do speak with the manager, don't ask "Are you hiring dealers?" The answer will almost always be "No." Instead, say something like "I would like to audition for a dealer's position." If the response is "We're not hiring right now," you can still ask "Would it be possible to audition anyway, so you can tell me if there's anything I need to work on?" Now you are requesting a favor. It never hurts to have an expert watch and give advice. And, you may impress him/her enough to be hired in the near future or to get on the extra board. At the very least you gain the experience of an audition so you won't be as nervous the next time.

Be prepared to answer several questions, including where you studied, how long the course was, and so forth. Also, be prepared in case the manager decides to audition you immediately. If the manager is interested, he will probably tell you to go to Personnel (or Human Resources), fill out an application, and bring a copy of the application back to the cardroom. (Don't bother the manager with questions like "Where is Personnel?" Ask a security guard or another non-cardroom employee.) If the cardroom manager says "I'll call you," you may or may not hear from him. However, if a week goes by you can always check back to see if there is any interest.

Filling out an Application

Some casinos require going to the Personnel department first. In such a case, going to the cardroom manager first may jeopardize your chances of being hired, so find out before you go.

When you fill out a job application you will need quite a bit of information. Be sure you have it with you. This includes, but may not be limited to:

1. Your full legal name and any aliases you may have used
2. Some form of photo identification, such as a driver's license
3. If not a U.S. citizen, any special ID cards, work permit, passport, etc.
4. Your social security card
5. If married, your spouse's full name and social security number
6. A history of your education, from junior high school up
7. Any special training you've had (e.g., a dealer's school)
8. A complete job history for the last five years (sometimes longer)
9. Your gaming card number (if you already have one)
10. Any convictions (other than minor traffic offenses)
11. At least two personal references and possibly professional references.

Be sure you have the complete name, address, telephone number, name of supervisor or instructor, and beginning and ending dates for every school, employer, and reference. Be complete. They *will* check some of the information on your application, and they will do a search for criminal records (even in other states). Most casinos will hire a person in spite of some minor offenses, but you will almost certainly be terminated if they find out you falsified or deliberately omitted information on your application.

Pens supplied in Personnel offices are often the cheapest kind, so you may want to take along your own pen to fill out the application (be sure it's black ink). Also, as previously stated, be professionally dressed (and clean), ready for an interview. In some casinos you will be interviewed by the Personnel department before going for an audition.

Going for an Audition

When going for an audition, it's important not to be late. Better yet, you should arrive early enough to observe other dealers for procedures that may be unique to that room. Again, be professionally dressed and properly groomed. Specifically:

1. Don't be smoking or chewing gum as you enter the cardroom.
2. Be neatly groomed — men freshly shaven.
3. Make sure your hair is an acceptable length and style.
4. Have clean, manicured nails (polished if desired).
5. Wear neat, pressed clothing.
6. Be sure to wear polished shoes (preferably black).
7. Have fresh breath, but nothing in your mouth.
8. Make sure there is nothing in your shirt pockets.
9. Don't wear a "fanny pack" or a large, fancy belt buckle.
10. Never take a friend or relative into the cardroom with you.
11. Don't carry a beeper or cellular phone (or at least turn them off).

Regardless of any special shirt, casual dress, or uniform worn in that particular cardroom, you should be professionally dressed in full "black and whites" when applying for a job. That is, black pants, socks, and shoes, and a plain white long-sleeved dress shirt with one pocket on the left side. A black bow tie is optional; in some cases an open collar is fine. For most cardrooms, a woman may substitute a black skirt (not too short) and nylons for the black pants and socks and may carry a purse (put it between your feet when you're in the box). Also, a woman may have better luck finding a suitable shirt in the men's department since women's blouses seldom have a pocket.

You should be fully prepared to sit down in the box and deal two or three hands, possibly hold 'em but probably stud. It goes without saying that you will be nervous. The manager knows this and will make allowances for it. Speed is of secondary importance.

Just do everything that's required, and do it accurately. Take control of the game just as if you had been doing it for years. Some players will recognize that you're auditioning, but they don't know whether you're a break-in or have ten years experience. However, they do know that you're handling *their* money.

Any tokes you receive during the audition go in your shirt pocket as usual. Don't forget, however, that those tokes would probably have been received by the regular dealer if you hadn't temporarily taken his or her place. It would be a nice gesture to offer the tokes to the regular dealer when you get up. It will probably be refused, but if you're hired to work on the same shift you have avoided a potential adversary. You came for an audition to get a job, not to make a couple dollars at another dealer's expense.

Starting on the Job

If you are hired, you will probably be required to take a drug test. Typically, they will want a urine sample and hair clippings. You may even be given a general physical exam. You will not have to pay for these tests.

In some cardrooms you may immediately be given a full-time shift. Be prepared for the possibility that you will be started on graveyard shift, which may start at 1:00, 2:00, or 3:00 am, depending on the casino. In other rooms you will be started either as a chiprunner or as a dealer on the "extra board."

A chiprunner does nothing but get fills, soft breaks, and other odd jobs around the room. Usually the regular dealers are expected to toke the chiprunner (perhaps $2 per shift from each dealer). The chiprunner may occasionally be allowed to deal if the cardroom is short of dealers. Also, a swing-shift chiprunner may be allowed to stay overtime and deal for awhile if there are not enough graveyard shift dealers for the games still in progress.

An extra board dealer does not come in at a preassigned time but is expected to be available whenever a shift manager needs an extra dealer. However, you can go to the room whenever you think it might be busy enough to be put to work. Besides getting to deal more often than the extra board dealer who just waits for a call, this show of *dependability* may help you to get on a regular shift.

Do not feel put upon if you are started as a chiprunner or extra board. It is probably standard procedure for that cardroom. If insurance is important to you, ask Personnel if part-time work counts toward qualifying for insurance or how long you have to be on full time to get it.

Whatever time you are supposed to start, be clocked in and ready ten or fifteen minutes early. This is because the line is usually pushed at least five minutes early at shift change, and the shift manager needs time before that to set up the new dealer lineup.

In most jurisdictions, each person working in a gaming facility must wear an identifying badge. Also, your gaming card must be carried on your person. It might be attached to your badge or in your wallet, but not in your locker or in your car. *You cannot work without it.*

Many casinos provide a decorative name tag that must be worn at all times while on the job.

Many casinos do not allow employees to smoke within view of the customers.

Getting a Gaming Card

Often called a sheriff's card or police card, everyone who works where there is gambling must have a gaming card. You must get an application form from the casino where you are being hired, signed by an authorized person — usually someone in Personnel or the casino manager.

In Las Vegas, you go to the downtown Metro Police Station (corner of Fremont and Sixth Street), take a number, and be prepared to spend $20.00 cash (no bigger bills) and several hours. The police station accepts reservations for renewals but not for your first card. In other jurisdictions, whoever gives you the application will tell you where to go to get your gaming card and what it will cost.

A few minutes after you've had your photo and fingerprints taken, you will probably be issued your regular card. However, if any criminal background is found, you may be refused a card or issued a temporary card. If things check out okay after a background check is completed, you will probably receive your regular card in the mail.

Tell your cardroom manager when you have received your regular card. For more detailed information on looking for a dealer job and getting a gaming card in Las Vegas, you may wish to refer to the book *Las Vegas Casino Employment Guide* by Lisa Alper (Jordan Publishing, $12.95).

Shifts

We recommend that, if asked, you readily agree to work any shift and any days. It's difficult enough to get a job without letting personal convenience interfere.

Nearly all casinos have three shifts. Graveyard is generally the first shift of the day, starting at 1:00, 2:00, or 3:00 am. Day shift begins eight hours after graveyard, and swing shift eight hours later. Shifts in other departments and in some large cardrooms are often staggered to reduce congestion in the parking lot and at the time clock.

You should be clocked in and present in the cardroom ten minutes before your shift starts so the shift manager can schedule the new lineup. Be in full uniform and ready to push the line at least five minutes before the shift starts.

Some casinos with only one or two poker tables don't spread poker on all shifts. The casino may start a game in the afternoon and close the cardroom whenever the last game breaks up. This might be done as one or two shifts.

Do's and Don'ts

Some final thoughts about things you should always do, things you should avoid, and other things you should never do:

Always...

1. Thank a player for a toke immediately, no matter how big or how small.
2. Put accuracy, technique, and efficiency ahead of speed.
3. Deal *to the* players. Do not make them reach for their cards.
4. Keep your full attention on the game. Your job is to run the game.
5. Announce any raise immediately. Then count the chips if necessary.
6. Make each announcement clear and concise.
7. Bring in the bets and get the final rake before reading hands.
8. Only maintain conversation necessary to running the game.
9. Push the pot directly to the winner. (Don't sweep too close to other player's money, and don't make the winner reach for it.)
10. Treat all the players the same. Race, color, creed, and gender are all equal.
11. Be clocked in and ready to deal at least fifteen minutes before your shift starts.
12. Push your line on time. Remember, the last dealer's break will be affected if you are late.
13. Be sure a mucked hand cannot be identified or retrieved from the muck.
14. Call the floorperson for a decision whenever needed. (Remember to always announce your table number.)
15. Once you call a floorperson, do only (and exactly) what is asked of you.
16. Be a professional.

Avoid...

1. Reading hands starting with "We have." (You are not part of "we." Worse, someone might get the idea that you are in collusion with a player.)
2. Reading hands starting with "It looks like." (Of course it "looks like" what you're about to say, or you wouldn't be saying it. Just state the value of the hand.)
3. Other redundant phrases such as "Okay...", "The bet is...", "It's on the...", "The action is...," or "It costs you...,". Be concise.
4. Flip comments such as "Last ticket to Sundown," "Last chance to bluff," or "I deal a winner every hand."
5. Being late for work. Allow time for a flat tire, etc. If you can't make it to work due to an emergency, call as soon as possible.
6. Any unnecessary conversation while in the box.
7. Delaying the game to count the bank. Get that first hand out immediately, and count the bank as time permits.

Never...

1. Borrow money while on the job.
2. Lend money while on the job. This includes other employees and customers. (New dealers are prime targets.)
3. Show any reaction to players, their cards, or their actions. For example:
   A. Refrain from exclaiming "Wow" when you flop three cards to a royal.
   B. Don't say "That's a hold 'em card" when a rag comes on the river.
   C. Don't make it obvious that you notice that a low is impossible in Omaha.
   D. Don't overemphasize a seven-card stud up card, as in "Three queens!"
4. Interrupt the shuffle sequence (even to pick up a toke).

5. Tell a player he "must" do something. (The player always has options.)
6. Get involved in an argument. (Call the floorperson.)
7. Second-guess the floorperson or discuss the decision at the table.
8. Turn a player's cards face up (unless *you* just turned them down).
9. Assist a player in the play of a hand. (Give only generic information.)
10. Make derogatory remarks about a player or how a hand was played.
11. Bring your personal problems to the table.
12. Worry about the time. (For example, notify a floorperson discreetly if you have not been pushed.)
13. Put anything on top of the muck. (Mix it into the "messy" pile.)
14. Put a card back on top of the deck unless an additional card was dealt in error. (Make sure the players understand your action.)
15. Point with your finger. (Point with your eyes or with an open hand.)
16. Say "Raise it up." (Has anyone ever raised it down? Just say "Raise.")
17. Argue with the floorperson. (If you disagree discuss it away from the table.)
18. Quit during your shift. You may have trouble getting another job anywhere in the industry. (Quitting at the end of a shift is marginally acceptable.)
19. Show up under the influence of drugs or alcohol, or use them while at work. (Note: Some casinos have random drug tests.)
20. Think you can get away with stealing from the casino, the pot, the players, or anyone or anywhere else. The cardroom managers usually know all the tricks, and cameras are everywhere. Even the smallest amount may result in termination and permanent loss of your gaming card. (Also, any amount may be prosecuted as a felony in Nevada.)

Appendix A
Course Outline

Besides being a useful guide for dealers and players, *The Professional Poker Dealer's Handbook* can also be used as the mandatory reading material for a poker dealing course. When this is the case we suggest that the course be structured into three parts or phases as shown below. If this text is used in this fashion, a written test may be administered and a practical evaluation may be given at the end of each part.[56] If a test is given it should include vocabulary (related terms from the glossary) and may include questions related to previous parts. Allow each practical evaluation to cover everything taught up to that point. This way the student cannot run the risk of becoming lazy on any skills just because he or she has already been evaluated on them. A dealer will need all the skills included in this handbook on the job. If a student receives a low mark on an early evaluation encourage the student to view this as an opportunity to improve.

Part 1: (About 35 hours class time)

General information (taken mostly from this handbook):
  Poker as played in public cardrooms
  General rules and procedures common to all games
  Poker terminology (see the glossary)

---

[56]See "A Note from Two Plus Two" at the beginning of this book for more information.

Basic mechanical skills (demonstration and lots of practice):[57]
> Scramble and shuffle cards, cut, release, and place deck in hand
>
> Pitch cards (face down and face up), burn cards, spread the flop
>
> Cut chips, stack chips, make change, handle the muck

Seven-card stud learned from the player's viewpoint
Texas hold 'em learned from the player's viewpoint
Player buy-ins, cash on table, selling chips, coloring up
Raises, minimum amount of a raise, string bets, and string raises
Reading hands (seven-card stud and Texas hold 'em)
Dealing seven-card stud and Texas hold 'em (no rake, no side pots)
Controlling the game (calling out the action, announcing all bets and raises, "option" to the blind, number of players, "last card," etc.)

Part 2: (About 30 hours class time)

Changing dealers, table lineup, break tables
Dealer's bank organization, counting the bank, getting a fill
Oversize chips, changing cash, soft breaks, when quarters play
Keeping track of total money in the pot, taking the rake at 5 percent
All-in bets, one side pot, raking the side pot
Structured limits, partial all-in bets, completing the bet
Straddles, missed blinds, dead button, dead blinds, dead money
Counting down the stub (seven-card stud and Texas hold 'em)
Getting a setup, spreading the deck
Error correction, when to call a floorperson

Part 3: (About 35 hours class time)

Pacing the game (keeping it moving without rushing the players)

---

[57]The objective is to make good habits of all necessary mechanical skills so that there is no need to think about them while dealing. That leaves your mind free for running the game.

Rake at 10 percent as specified on some games[58]
Multiple side pots, deferring rake on small side pots
Protecting the pot, protecting the players
Foreign chips, slot tokens, oversize chips, etc.
Playing behind, betting "on the piece"
Omaha, Omaha high-low split, stacking the pot, reading hands
Jackpot rake, jackpot procedures
Going for an audition, getting started on the job

Suggested total classroom time is one hundred hours, but the student is expected to study the manual on his or her own time (especially through the first test and evaluation). Some students may be ready for an audition in less than 100 hours, and others will take longer. This depends partially on manual dexterity, but more on diligence and enthusiasm.

---

[58]It is suggested that the 5 percent rake be learned before 10 percent. This gets the student into the habit of thinking in terms of units (e.g., one quarter rake for each $5 in the pot) rather than percentages. It's much quicker to figure in units than to calculate percentage.

Appendix B
Glossary of Poker Terms

Many terms are unique to poker, and many poker terms have found a place in common language. Following are most of the terms you are likely to hear in a cardroom. Terms noted as "slang" generally should not be used by a dealer, at least within the hearing of players.

Absent button: A chip-size marker put at a player's stack of chips when a new dealer sits down and the player is not at the table.

Ace: A card with one pip. Usually considered to be the highest card of a suit, it also may be used to make a five-high straight. In lowball it's the lowest card except in deuce-to-seven where an ace is always high.

Action: (1) Any check, bet, raise, call, or fold by any player. (2) Any partial bet, raise, or call by a player going all-in; (3) The betting in a particular hand or game. A game with a lot of action is a game with a lot of betting. The player who starts the action is the player who takes the first action.

Active player: A player still in the pot.

Add-on: A one-time add-on buy may be offered at the end of the rebuy period in a tournament.

All-in: Having all one's money on the table in the pot.

Ante: A bet required from all players before the start of a hand.

Back door: A hand made on the end, which a player was not originally trying to make.

Bad beat: Having a hand that is a big favorite defeated as the result of a lucky draw.

Bank: The money and chips contained in the rack in front of the dealer. (See also **rack**.)

Bankroll: The amount of money a player has available to wager. (See also **stake**.)

Being staked: A player who is put in action by one or more backers is said to be "staked."

Belly buster: A draw to an inside straight. Also called a **gut shot.**

Best of it: A situation in which a wager can be expected to be profitable in the long run.

Bet: (v) To put money in the pot before anyone else on any given round; (n) The amount of such a wager.

Betting area: The central area of the table where, if a player places any chips or money, it is taken as a bet or raise. If a player releases his cards face down in this area it is taken as a fold. (Unfortunately this area is often poorly defined.)

Betting round: A complete wagering cycle. It's finished when all active players have checked or all have placed the same amount of money into the pot (or, if going all-in, all the money they have on the table).

Bettor: The person who first puts money in the pot on any given round.

Bicycle: Ace, 2, 3, 4, 5 — the best possible hand in lowball. Also called a **wheel** and a **baby straight.** The term is used in all games.

Big slick: In hold 'em, an ace and a king in the hole (slang).

Blank: A card that is not of any value to a player's hand.

Blind: In hold 'em, draw lowball, and some other games, a forced bet that one or more players must make to start the action on the first round of betting. The blind rotates around the table with each new deal. The person whose turn it is to post this bet is said to be "in the blind."

Blue: Slang for a club or spade flush ("All blue").

Bluff: A bet or raise with a hand that the player does not think is the best hand.

Board: The cards that are face up in a player's hand. In hold 'em, the community cards.

Board game: Any game played with cards appearing face up.

Bottom: A cheating move that entails dealing the bottom card of the deck.

Bottom pair: Making a pair by having a card in one's hand of the same rank as the lowest rank card on the board.

Box: (n) The dealer's position at the table, including the rack; (v) To strip-shuffle the cards.

Boxed card: A card that is found to be face up in the deck. A boxed card is usually treated as a piece of paper.

Break-in: An inexperienced dealer.

Break-in house: A casino that will hire inexperienced dealers.

Break table: The last table dealt before going on break.

Bring-in: A forced bet, as on the low door card in seven-card stud.

Bring it in: To start the betting on the first round. (See also **open**.)

Broken game or **broken table:** A game that ended because of too few players. (The floorperson usually tries to move the players into other active games.)

Brush: (n) A cardroom employee whose duties include keeping a list and seating players in the games (in many small rooms this function is performed by a floorperson or by dealers on break); (v) To clean a table.

Bug: The joker.

Bullets: Aces (slang).

Burn: The top card off the deck is "burned" face down under a chip in the pot before each round of dealing after the first. This is to protect the players in case there might be an identifiable mark on the back of the card.

Busted hand: A hand that does not develop into anything of value.

Bust out: A dealer who receives "last break" may be able to leave work a half hour or twenty minutes early depending on your cardroom policy. However, never assume this. Always check with the floorperson.

Button: When there is a house dealer, as in the cardrooms of Las Vegas, the *button* is a round disc that rotates around the table to represent the dealer for the purposes of indicating which player is to be first to act. A button is necessary in hold 'em, draw lowball, and five-card draw. (See also the section on other buttons in the text.)

Buy-in: The minimum amount of money required to sit down in a particular game. (See also **stake**.)

Cardroom: The area in a casino where poker (and sometimes panguingue or "pan" for short) are played.

Cage: The casino cashier. (So called because there usually are bars on the windows.)

Call: To put in the pot an amount of money equal to an opponent's bet or raise.

Caller: A player who calls a bet or raise.

Calling station: A player who calls virtually all bets but seldom raises (slang).

Cap: (1) The last allowed raise during the current betting round. (2) The maximum rake has been reached.

Card party: A *requested* gathering of dealers on break to make up setups, when necessary. *Come when invited.*

Cards speak: If all of a player's cards are turned face up by that player at the time of the showdown then the best possible hand plays regardless of how it might have been called. It is the dealer's responsibility to read each player's hand and push the pot to the player with the best hand, but it is the cards themselves that determine the value of a hand. Anyone may point out errors in reading a hand.

Case card: The last available card of any given rank. For example, you need a jack to fill an inside straight, but three of them are showing in other players' hands; the remaining unseen jack is the case jack.

Cash out: When a player leaves the game and converts his chips back to cash, usually either at the poker cage or casino cage. (The dealer may not take cash from his rack to do this, but may *color up* the player to higher denomination chips.)

Cash plays: In many (but not all) cardrooms, any cash on the table is considered to be part of the player's stake. It can be exchanged for chips at any time, even in the middle of a hand, or it can be bet and the dealer will make change. In some rooms cash is not allowed on the table, or even if allowed it does not play until converted to chips.

Check: (n) A chip with a monetary value. (v) To decline to bet when it is your turn (if there has already been a bet, a player may not check but must either call, raise, or fold).

Check out: To fold one's hand when there has been no bet. (That is, the player could have just checked.)

Check-raise: To check and then raise after an opponent bets.

Chip: A round token that may have any of various uses. A chip representing money is also called a check.

Chiprunner: A cardroom employee whose duties include getting fills for the dealers, getting soft breaks, and player's checks. In small rooms, this function is usually performed by a floorperson or by dealers who are on break.

Chop-chop: Split the pot (slang).

Cinch: The best possible hand, given the cards on board, when all the cards are out. (See also **nuts** and **lock**.)

Clear the deck: This refers to the requirement that the dealer take both hands clear of the deck before cutting the cards.

Closed hand: A hand in which all the cards are concealed from one's opponents, as in draw poker.

Color up: To give a player higher denomination chips in exchange for small denomination chips.

Come hand: A hand that has not yet been made, with more cards still to be dealt. Thus, a four-card flush would be a come hand.

Community cards: The five faceup cards (board cards) in the center of the table in hold 'em or Omaha. Community cards are used by each player as part of his hand. Occasionally there might be a community card in seven-card stud if too few cards remain to give each player a seventh card.

Complete the bet: To put out a full bet when there has been a partial bet (usually because another player went all-in for less than half the required bet). This applies in a structured-limit game or when a minimum bet has been established by an earlier bet in the same round.

Contract dealer: A dealer who travels around dealing mostly major tournaments.

Counterfeited: One or more of a player's low cards is duplicated on the board, often ruining a low hand (especially in Omaha).

Cover card: A non-playing card used to cover the bottom of the deck, usually a plain plastic card. Some rooms use the joker as a cover card. (See also **cut card.**)

Cowboys: Kings (slang).

Crab: A card of rank three, properly called a "trey" (slang).

Crying call: A call with a hand that appears to have only a small chance of winning.

Cut: (v) To cut the cards (see also **cut card**); (n) In a tournament, being one of the players to remain in the event when tables are combined, as in "I made the cut to the last table."

Cut card: Same as the **cover card.** It is not used to cut the deck, although the deck is cut *onto* the cut card by the dealer.

Cut the pot: To take a percentage from each pot as the fee for the casino (see also **rake**).

Dead blind: A blind that is designated to a seat that is not now occupied, so that blind is not posted. (See also **missed blind** and **dead money.**)

Dead button: The dealer button is advanced to a seat that is not now occupied. Some cardrooms use an "advancing button rule" which prevents this situation.

Dead game: A game with little or no significant action.

Dead hand: A hand a player may not continue to play because of an irregularity. (See also **fouled hand.**)

Dead money: (1) Money put in the pot by players who have already folded their hands; (2) The small blind portion of a make-up blind.

Dead spread: A table with a dealer and bank but no game being dealt.

Dealer's choice: Poker in which the player whose turn it is to deal may choose the game for that particular hand.

Dealer's room: A break room. (See also **help's hall.**)

Decision: What is called for whenever a dispute or irregularity occurs. Example: "Decision table number 10."

Deuce: A card of rank two. There are no "twos" in a poker deck, always deuces.

Deuce-to-seven: A form of poker usually played as a seven-card stud or draw lowball game where aces are high and straights and flushes count against the hand. The best hand is 7-5-4-3-2.

Dime: Ten dollars (slang). In a high-stakes room, a "dime" might mean one thousand dollars.

Dirty stack: A stack of chips containing one or more chips of a different denomination.

Discard: (v) The act of releasing one's hand with a forward motion; the dealer should immediately slide the cards into the muck (see also **fold**); (n) Any card or hand that has been discarded.

Don't shoot: In a heads-up situation, one player may discard his hand saying "Don't shoot" when it appears that the other player is about to bet.

Door card: In stud games, the first face up card in a player's hand.

Double gutshot: An inside straight draw that can be completed at either of two points. When you hold 10,8,7,6,4 either a 9 or a 5 will give you a straight. Also called a **double belly buster** or **double gutbuster.**

Double nuts: The best possible hand for both high and low in high-low split games. (See also **nut-nut.**)

Down: A dealer's twenty or thirty minutes dealing at one table.

Draw: (v) To take one or more cards; (n) A form of poker in which each player receives five cards and then has the option of discarding one or more of them and receiving new cards in their place.

Drawing dead: Drawing to try to make a hand that cannot possibly win because an opponent already holds a bigger hand. A player drawing to make a flush when an opponent already has a full house is drawing dead.

Draw lowball: A form of poker in which the lowest hand wins.

Draw out: To improve a hand so that it beats an opponent who had a better hand prior to your draw.

Drop box: A locked box under the table that catches the rake when it's dropped. There may be a second box for a jackpot rake.

Ducks: Deuces (slang).

Early position: A position on a round of betting in which you must act before *most* of the other players.

Eight-or-better: Required to qualify as a low hand in most high-low split games. The player must have five cards of different ranks that are all eight or lower. (The ace is counted as a low card.)

Eighty-six: To ban a person from a casino or from a particular game.

Exposed card: Any card whose face was seen by one or more players who should not have seen it. (See also **boxed card** which should not be confused with an exposed card; they are different and are treated differently.)

Extra board: A dealer who has not been assigned a regular shift but is on call when needed is said to be "on the extra board."

Eye in the sky: Cameras that observe all games in a casino.

Family pot: All players at the table called the bet and are still in the pot (slang).

Favorite: In poker, before all the cards are out, a hand that has the best chance of winning.

Feeler: A bet made to see what the other players will do. (See also **nuisance raise.**)

Fifth street: In stud poker, the fifth card to be dealt to each player. In hold 'em the fifth and final community card on board. (See also **river.**)

Fill: (1) The exchange of cash and/or foreign chips from a dealer's rack for the proper number of each denomination of chips to fill the rack correctly (see also **chiprunner** and **lammer**.); (2) To draw or catch a card that makes a hand. For example, to fill a flush is to receive a fifth card of that suit.

Fill up: To make a full house.

Finn: A $5 bill; also known as a **nickel** (slang).

First break: A dealer that is on break during the first down of his or her shift.

Fish: A player who lacks many poker skills.

Fixed limit: Same as **structured limit.**

Flat call: To call a bet without raising.

Flat limit: A betting limit in a poker game that does not escalate from one round to the next.

Floorperson: (1) A cardroom employee whose duties include seeing that the room is run in an orderly fashion; also makes decisions in case of an argument, uncorrectable dealer error, or questionable circumstances in any game; (2) Sometimes brush people are called floorpersons, but they rarely make decisions. (See also **supervisor** and **shift manager.**)

Flop: (1) In hold 'em or Omaha the first three community cards, which are dealt face up simultaneously; (2) To make a hand on the flop; for example, to flop a set is to make three-of-a-kind on the flop; (3) The act by the dealer of putting up the flop.

Flop game: Any game with community board cards, such as hold 'em or Omaha.

Flop lag: A player's lament that this flop is what he needed for the previous hand.

Flush: Five cards of the same suit.

Fold: To drop out of a pot rather than call a bet or raise.

Forced bet: A required bet to start the action on the first round of a poker hand. In seven-card stud, the low card on board must make a forced bet.

Foreign check: A chip from another casino.

Fouled hand: A hand that contains an improper number of cards or has come in contact with other cards while unprotected. Such a hand is usually declared dead. (See also **dead hand.**)

Four flush: Four cards to a flush.

Four-of-a-kind: Four cards of the same rank. Four jacks is four-of-a-kind.

Fourth street: In stud games, the fourth card dealt to each player. In hold 'em, the fourth community card on board.

Fourth street rule: When this seven-card stud rule is in effect, any player has the option of making a higher limit bet if an open pair shows in any hand on fourth street. (Applies to structured-limit or mixed-limit games only.)

Free card or **free ride:** A card that a player gets without having to call a bet.

Free roll: (1) A tournament where players receive their buy-in by playing a certain minimum number of hours in the cardroom's live games during the preceding week or month; Players with more hours recorded may receive more starting chips; rebuys are usually not allowed; (2) A poker hand with more cards to come that has the same (current) value as an opposing hand, but also has the potential to improve while the opposing hand does not.

Freeze out: A game or tournament event in which the players involved continue play until only one player has all the chips.

Friday: The last day of one's work week. The gambling industry is a seven-day-a-week business, so each employee's work week may start on a different day of the calendar week. If you are off on Tuesday and Wednesday, then Monday on the calendar is your "Friday," and Thursday is your "Monday."

Full boat: Full house (slang).

Full house: Three cards of one rank and two of another. For example, three aces and two 10s is a full house.

Gallery: An area from which an audience is allowed to watch a poker game or tournament.

Game bank: A specific amount of chips brought to the table for the express purpose of starting a game.

Gaming card: The card issued by the sheriff's office or local police which must be carried on your person while at work in a gaming establishment. (See also **sheriffs card.**)

George: A player who tokes generously (slang).

Ghost hand: Due to a poor shuffle, a sequence of cards from the previous hand appears.

Going south: Refers to a player taking money or chips off the table while still playing in the game. (See also **rat hole.**)

Grind: To slowly make a profit playing poker, usually in low-limit games.

Grind joint: A cardroom that offers low-limit games where a regular can "grind out" a small profit.

Gutshot: A draw to an inside straight. Also called a **belly buster.**

Half kill: The betting limits are increased by 50 percent instead of doubled. (See also **kill.**)

Hammer: Having the button, thus being last to act, which puts the player in a strategically strong position.

Hand: (1) Any player's cards; (2) The complete play of a hand of poker, from shuffle and deal through all betting rounds and the showdown.

Heads-up: Only two players remain in action.

Helicopter: To pitch a player's card high and spinning. (This is an undesirable show-off move). (See also **snapping and spinning.**)

Help's hall: The employees' cafeteria. (See also **dealer's room.**)

High-low split: A form of poker in which the best high hand and the best low hand split the pot. Usually this game is played with a *qualifier* for low. (See also **Eight-or-better.**)

Hold 'em: Also called Texas hold 'em. An increasingly popular form of poker in which players use five community cards in combination with their two hole cards to form the best five-card hand.

Hold 'em card: A turn or river card that doesn't appear likely to affect what's to be the winning hand. (See also **blank**.)

Hole cards: In seven-card stud games, the first two concealed cards. In five-card stud games, the first and only concealed card. In hold 'em, the player's two cards. In Omaha, the player's four cards.

Home game: A poker game held in someone's home or club.

Hooks: Jacks (slang).

HORSE: A table where the game rotates through hold 'em, Omaha high-low split eight-or-better, razz, seven-card stud, and seven-card stud eight-or-better, usually changing after a specified number of hands, usually eight or ten.

HOSE: HORSE without razz.

Hot sucker: A player who lost a big pot who now plays very poorly (slang). (See also **on tilt** and **steaming**.)

Hot sucker raise: A raise almost certainly made due to being a "hot sucker."

Hourly rate: The amount of money a player expects to win per hour on average.

Human Resources: The Personnel department.

Inside straight: A straight that can be made only with a card of one rank, usually somewhere in the middle of the straight. When you hold 10,9,7,6 only an 8 will give you a straight. Thus, you are drawing to an inside straight, or you have an inside-straight draw. (See also **gut shot.**)

Jackpot: Some cardrooms have a "bad beat" jackpot that's paid when a hand of a certain minimum high value loses to an even better hand. Other rooms may have different kinds of jackpots, such as for holding a specific hand, high hand of the day, etc.

Jacks-or-better to open: Draw poker in which a player needs at least a pair of jacks to start the betting.

Jam the pot: Excessive bets and raises by one or more players.

Jam-up game: A game where several players are building very large pots, often with little regard to hand values.

Joker: The fifty-third card in the deck, used only in specific games. In lowball draw, it is the lowest card not already in a player's hand. In high draw, it is either an ace or can be used to complete straights or flushes. (Typically, in public cardrooms, the joker is only used in forms of draw poker.)

Kicker: (1) In hold 'em, a nonmatching card that is used to determine the winner when two hands are otherwise equal, usually with one or two pair; (2) In stud, a side card, usually a high one; someone holding 9,9,A has a pair of 9s with an ace *kicker;* (3) In draw poker, a high card (usually an ace) held with a pair.

Kill: Depending on house rules, a player is allowed or required to "kill" the pot under certain circumstances in some games, thus doubling the betting limits for that hand. There may be a "kill button" involved. (See also **half kill.**)

Knock: Tapping the table to indicate a check.

Ladies: Queens (slang).

Lammers: Numbered disks used to indicate the amount missing from the dealer's rack when getting a fill. Typically they are slightly larger than a quarter and a different color for each value.

Last break: A dealer is on break during what would be the last down of his or her shift. (See also **bust-out.**)

Late position: A position on a round of betting in which a player acts after most of the other players have acted.

Legitimate hand: A hand with value; a hand that is not a bluffing hand.

Let 'em live: "Check" (slang, by big blind).

Light: (1) A player does not have enough money to call a bet but is playing behind (where this is allowed); (2) The pot is short. (See also **playing behind.**)

Limit: The amount a player may bet or raise on any round of betting.

Limit poker: A poker game where the minimum and maximum amounts a player may bet or raise on any given round of betting are fixed.

Limits: The minimum and maximum bet sizes allowed at various times through a hand. (See also **spread limit, structured limit, mixed limit, pot limit,** and **no-limit.**)

Limp-in: To just call the bet, often with a low probability drawing hand. (See also **smooth call.**)

Lineup: (1) The sequence of tables for a dealer to go through; (2) The assignment of dealers to certain tables; (3) The players in a poker game.

Live blind: A blind bet that acts as part or all of a player's bet. The player who posted it has the option to raise when the action reaches that seat (unless the raises have been capped), or he may check if there has been no raise. (See also **straddle.**)

Live card: In stud games, a card that has not yet been seen and is therefore presumed likely to be still available.

Live hand: Any player's hand that is still in contention for any part of the pot.

Live one: A loose, weak player with a lot of money to lose. A rich sucker. There is a story, perhaps apocryphal, about a poker game in Gardena in which one player had a heart attack and died. The player to his left shouted to the floorman, "Hey, Louie, bring us a live one."

Lock: A cinch hand, but not necessarily the "nuts." A hand that cannot lose. For example, if the board is

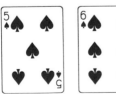  

then a player holding

has a lock because he knows that no one can make the straight flush. The "nuts" is a definition, and it is

in this case, even though at showdown we see that such a holding was impossible.

Locksmith: A player who plays a hand only if it is almost certain to be the winner (slang).

Long odds: The odds for an event that has a relatively small chance of occurring.

Long shot: An event that has little chance of occurring. Hence, in poker a hand that has little chance of being made.

Loose: Playing more hands than proper strategy would call for, or being a very liberal bettor, raiser, or caller.

Loose game or **loose table:** A game with several loose players.

Lowball: A variety of poker in which the lowest hand wins in the showdown. Depending on the game rules, a straight or flush may or may not be detrimental to the value of a hand, and a joker may or may not be used. (See also **deuce-to-seven.**)

Main pot: The first pot formed in each hand. It is simply "the pot" until a player goes all-in, causing a side pot to be formed.

Mechanic: A dealer who is highly skilled at stacking the deck or cheating by other card manipulations. Since the casino dealer does not actually play in the game, the cheating is usually done to favor a partner who is playing. (See also **bottom, peek, second, stacking,** and **topping.**)

Middle position: A position on a round of betting somewhere in the middle. In a ten-handed game, the fourth, fifth, and sixth players to act would be said to be in middle position.

Misdeal: The cards are all taken back, reshuffled, and redealt. Criteria for declaring a misdeal depend upon house rules.

Missed blind button: A chip-sized marker placed by the dealer at a player's chips when the player does not post a blind in turn, usually because the player is absent from the table. In a game with two blinds, there may be separate small blind and big blind buttons. A small blind button is given when the player has missed the small blind *only.*

Mixed limit: A spread-limit game where the betting structure allows a small spread on early streets and a larger spread on later streets.

Monday: The first day of one's work week. (See also **Friday.**)

Monster: A very strong hand.

Muck: (n) The discard pile; (v) To put cards into the muck.

Multiway pot: A pot in which more than two players are involved.

Move all-in: To bet all the money one has on the table.

Must move: A second game that is started to protect the first or main game. A player, upon his turn to move, must move or quit the game in which he is playing.

Nickel: Gamblers' slang for five dollars or a $5 chip. (See also **red bird.**) In a high-stakes room, a "nickel" may mean $500.

No-limit poker: Poker in which players may wager any amount up to what they have in front of them on any given round.

No qualifier: In a high-low split game with no qualifier the high and low hand will split the pot.

No vacancy: Full house (slang).

Nuisance bet or **nuisance raise:** A minimum bet or raise in a spread-limit game. (See also **feeler.**)

Nut-nut: A hand having both the "nut high" and the "nut low" in a high-low split game. Also called **double nuts.**

Nuts: The best possible holding at any given point in a hand.

Odd chip: An extra chip left after splitting a pot.

Odds: The chances, expressed mathematically, that an event will occur. Also, in the term **pot odds,** the ratio of the size of the pot to the amount of the bet a player must call to continue.

Off-suit: Not of the same suit.

On the clock: An employee being paid his or her hourly rate (as opposed to "off the clock" and thus on his or her own time).

On the come: Playing a hand that has not yet been made. For instance, if you bet with four cards to a flush, you are betting on the come.

On the piece: A player wishing to bet or call who has cash on the table but not enough chips may push out a bill and say "Put it on the piece." If house rules allow, the dealer will place chips from the pot "on the piece" to mark the amount.

On tilt: Playing much worse than usual because, for one reason or another, a player has become emotionally upset.

Open: To make the first bet in a poker hand. The term is used especially in draw poker.

Opener: (1) The player who "opens" the pot by making the first bet; (2) In draw poker, a hand consisting of a pair of jacks or better is usually required to open the betting.

Open-ended straight: Four cards to a straight, which can be made with cards of two different ranks. Thus

is an open-ended straight, which can be made with either a 5 or a 10. Effectively

is also open-ended in that either a 6 or a 10 will make the hand. The latter hand is also called a **double gutshot.**

Open game: Any game open to any player having the required buy-in (provided there is a seat available). Nearly all games in public cardrooms are open games. (See also **private game.**)

Open hand: The accepted way to signal a customer that the action is on them.

Open-handed: A poker game like seven-card stud or razz in which some cards in each player's hand are exposed.

Open pair: An exposed pair.

Open seat: A poker seat where there is no player, chips, or reserved button.

Option: If there has been no raise, then a player who has posted the big blind, or any required blind equal to the big blind, has the option to either check or raise when the action reaches that seat. No other player has the option to check.

Outs: Cards that will improve your hand. Also, ways of improving your hand. The term is used particularly in reference to a hand that needs to improve to become the best hand.

Outdraw: See **draw out.**

Overcard: (1) In stud games, a card higher than any card your opponent has showing; (2) In hold 'em games, a card higher than any card on board.

Overpair: A pocket pair higher than any of the cards on board.

Paint: Any face card (jack, queen, or king) (slang).

Pair: Two cards of the same rank. For example, two 8s is a pair.

Pass: To check, especially in draw poker. Also, to fold.

Pass through: A method of cheating by doing a false shuffle. Avoid suspicion by never obscuring the deck from the players' view. Use only the pinch to square up the deck.

Pat hand: In draw poker games, a complete hand before the draw. A pat flush would be a five-card flush before the draw.

Pay off: To call a bet or raise when you don't think you have the best hand.

Pay station: A player who calls bets and raises much more than is correct. He's also referred to as a **calling station.** This type is great when you have a legitimate hand, but he's just about impossible to bluff out of a pot.

Peek: A method of cheating by peeking at the top card when the deck is inverted. A professional dealer avoids suspicion by keeping the deck level. (See also **second** and **mechanic.**)

Penny: Gamblers' slang for one dollar or a $1 chip. In a high-stakes room, a "penny" may mean $100.

Pineapple: A variation of hold 'em where each player receives three cards down and discards one of them before the flop. In crazy pineapple, the discard is after the flop. A hand is fouled and will be declared dead if it contains three cards at showdown.

Pink: Slang for a heart or diamond flush ("all pink").

Pip: One of the spots on a playing card.

Play behind: A player takes a seat and announces how much he is playing without actually putting any money on the table. This is not allowed in most public cardrooms, but the term "playing behind" is sometimes used when the player has already given money to a chiprunner or floorperson and wants to begin playing immediately. In high-stakes games, playing behind is an agreement between players; the house rules are and should be table stakes. (See also **light.**)

Play over: A player leaves his chips on the table when taking a break; the floorperson counts the chips, then covers them (usually with a clear plastic box, a chip rack, or a towel) and allows another player to play in that seat until the original player returns. The new player is said to be "playing over" the original player.

Play the board: In hold 'em, a player whose best five cards are the community cards is said to be "playing the board."

Playing the rush: A player on a lucky streak, playing every hand, is said to be "playing the rush." (See also **rush.**)

Pocket: Another term for hole. Thus, two aces in the pocket means two aces in the hole.

Pocket rockets: A pair of aces in the hole, usually in hold 'em (slang).

Position: The spot in the sequence of betting in which a player is located. A player in first position would be the first person to act; a player in last position would be the last person to act.

Position bet: A bet made in a late position. May be trying to steal the pot since no one else has bet, or may have a strong hand and wants others to call, believing he's on the steal.

Possible: A hand that can be completed by one more card, as in a possible straight or possible flush, in a player's four upcards in seven-card stud.

Possible pair: A hand with no pair (disgruntled slang).

Post mortem: Discussion of a hand after play is complete, often in excruciating detail. (The dealer should avoid getting involved in any such discussion and try to keep the game moving.)

Pot: The total amount of money wagered at any point in a hand. A hand itself is also referred to as a pot. Thus, three people in the pot means there are three active players still playing the hand.

Pot limit poker: Poker in which players may bet or raise any amount up to the current size of the pot. The call portion of a player's wager is usually considered to be part of the pot for the purpose of determining the maximum raise.

Pot odds: The ratio of the amount of money in the pot to the bet you must call to continue in the hand.

Private game: A game that is not open to the public but only to specific players or by invitation. Usually very high stakes, and often in a separate room. Private games do sometimes occur, but are rare in public cardrooms. (See also **home game.**)

Professional gambler: One whose principal source of income (or intended income) is gambling.

Progression: In a tournament, the blinds and/or betting limits go up periodically according to a predetermined progression.

Prop: See **proposition player.**

Proper card: The card a player would receive if there were no procedural irregularities in the deal.

Proposition player: Often called a "prop" for short, this is a house employee who plays his or her own money in a game designated by the floorperson. Props are used to get games started or to keep a short game going.

Protected hand: The player is physically holding the cards or has placed one or more chips or some other object on top of the cards.

Pump: Raise, as in "Pump it up" (slang).

Puppy feet: Clubs, the suit (slang).

Push: The break dealer "pushes the line" by going to the first table in a line and tapping the dealer on the shoulder. At the end of the current hand, that dealer gets up and goes to the next table in the lineup to push that dealer. The last dealer in that line goes on break. (See also **lineup.**)

Put someone on a hand: A player determines as best he can the hand (or hands) an opponent is most likely to have.

Quads: Four of a kind (slang).

Qualifier: An eight-or-better is usually required to qualify as a low hand in a high-low split game with a qualifier. (See also **no qualifier.**)

Quartered: Receiving only one-quarter of the pot, most often due to a tie for low in a high-low split game.

Rabbit hunting: Looking at the burn cards or the stub of the deck to see what would have happened if the player had stayed in. This practice should be gently discouraged and is not allowed in many cardrooms.

Rack: (1) A device for carrying chips, usually holding one hundred chips in five stacks of twenty; (2) The tray in front of the dealer holding the dealer's bank.

Rag: A useless card. (See also **blank.**)

Rail bird: A wanna-be poker player standing at the rail and watching the game. Often trying to borrow money to get in a game.

Rainbow: (1) A stack of chips of mixed colors (See also **dirty stack.**); (2) A flop of three different suits.

Raise: To raise an additional amount after someone else has bet.

Raiser: A player who raises.

Rake or **rake off:** An amount retained by a casino from each pot. (See also **time** and **drop box.**)

Rank: The numerical value of a card: ace, deuce, trey, four, five, six, seven, eight, nine, ten, jack, queen, king.

Rat hole: A player who pockets chips from the table (usually surreptitiously), thus reducing his table stake, is said to be rat holing the chips. Many players rat hole coins, and usually nothing is said, but a player may not take chips or cash off the table unless he is leaving the game. (See also **going south.**)

Razz: Seven-card stud lowball. The original name of the game was "razzle dazzle."

Read: An experienced player tries to "read" the other players in an attempt to "put them on a hand."

Red bird: A $5 chip (regardless of its actual color). Less commonly used are "blue bird" (a $1 chip), "green bird" (a $25 chip), and "black bird" (a $100 chip). (See also **nickel.**)

Represent: To make an opponent believe there is a bigger hand than is showing on board. Thus, if in seven-card stud a player raises with an ace showing, he is representing a pair of aces. He may or may not in fact have a pair of aces.

Reraise: To raise after an opponent has raised.

Riffle: The intermingling of cards during the shuffle.

Ringer: (1) An expert player who acts like an amateur (slang); (2) An unknown player who plays very well.

River: The seventh and last card, dealt face down, in seven-card stud and razz. The fifth and last up card in hold 'em or Omaha.

Rock: A very conservative player. Similar to a **locksmith.**

Roll the deck: The *unacceptable* act of a dealer inverting the deck, usually when gathering bets into the pot or looking at his watch with the deck in his hand.

Rolled up: In seven-card stud, three-of-a-kind on the first three cards.

Rough: A lowball hand that is not perfect. Thus,

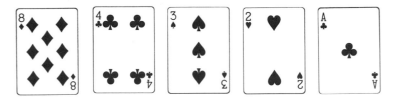

is a perfect eight. An

is a rough eight.

Round of betting: A sequence of betting after one or more cards have been dealt. A round of betting continues until each active player has either folded or called all bets — unless they are all-in.

Royal flush: An ace-high straight flush of any suit.

is a royal flush.

Runners: Any two consecutive cards that make a player's hand.

Running pair: Any two consecutive cards of the same rank, but especially the last two board cards in hold'em or Omaha.

Rush: A winning streak. Sometimes called a "run." (See **also playing the rush.**)

Sandbag: To play weakly with a strong hand. To check raise or slowplay with the probable best hand.

Sawbuck: A $10 bill (slang).

Scared money: Too small a bankroll for the stakes being played, or perhaps money that is needed for food or rent.

Scooper: A hand that wins the entire pot — in a high-low split game. Not to be confused with the nuts.

Score: A big win.

Scramble: To mix the cards by sliding them around on the table. Also called **washing the cards.**

Seat charge: In public cardrooms, an hourly fee for playing poker.

Second: A method of cheating by dealing the second card from the top of the deck. (See also **mechanic** and **peek.**)

Second nuts: The second best possible hand, followed by the third nuts, etc.

Semi-bluff: To bet with a hand that you do not think is the best hand but which has a reasonable chance of improving to the best hand.

Send it: A statement made by a player when showing the best hand (referring to the pot). Same as **ship it.**

Set: Three-of-a-kind. The term is used particularly in hold 'em.

Setup: Two fresh decks of cards, sorted by suit and rank.

Sevens rule: In lowball draw, a player holding a seven or better is required to bet, or else after the draw he is subject to losing further bets, but cannot win any additional money.

Seventh street: In seven-card stud games, the seventh card dealt to each player.

Sheriff's card: An identification card issued by the local police or sheriff. Nearly everyone working in any establishment where there is legal gambling is required to have such a card. Also called a "police card" or "gaming card."

Shift: One's work day, usually eight hours plus a little overlap with adjoining shifts.

Shift manager: Directly under the cardroom manager, this person is in charge of the room during one shift. In a small room, the shift manager may also be the only floorperson and/or brush.

Shill: A cardroom employee who uses house money instead of his or her own to fill a seat in a game. (A shill generally does not create any action or make any bets other than forced bets. Shills are rarely used anymore.) (See also **prop.**)

Ship it: "Push me the pot" — stated by a player who probably has the "nuts". (See also **send it.**)

Shoot out: A tournament event that is played down to one winner per table before advancing. (See also **freeze out.**)

Short buy: Less than a full buy-in. (In many cardrooms, a player is allowed one short buy per eight- hour playing session. This policy varies by cardroom.) In some cardrooms, to qualify as a short buy, it must be at least half of the original buy-in.

Short game: A table with several open seats.

Short stack: A stack of less than twenty chips.

Short-stacked: Playing in a game with a relatively small number of chips remaining.

Shorts: A draw poker term meaning a pair smaller than jacks (minimum openers).

Shovels: Spades, the suit (slang).

Showdown: The turning up of all active hands by the players at the end of the final round of betting to see who has the best hand. (See also **cards speak.**)

Showing clean hands: Whenever you put your hands in, near, or on the pot (to push it) come away with your palms open. Also, when leaving the table, lightly clap your hands and show them palms up.

Shuffle: (v) To rearrange the cards into a random order; (n) The riffle portion of the complete shuffle procedure.

Side bet: A bet other than on one's own poker hand. (For example, a player not in the action may offer to bet another such player about the hands still in action. Not allowed in most cardrooms, although it's very difficult to enforce.)

Side pot: A second pot for the other active players when one player is all-in.

Slowplay: To check or just call an opponent's bet with a big hand in order to win more money on later rounds of betting.

Smooth call: A player with a monster hand just calls instead of raising, hoping for more callers, perhaps with the intent of a later check-raise.

Snapped off: A term for having lost with a big starting hand (such as pocket aces in hold 'em or "rolled up trips" in seven-card stud).

Snatch game: Prior to Nevada gaming regulations setting the maximum rake at 10 percent in 1974, some cardrooms would rake their games up to 50 percent. These were known as "snatch games."

Social game: A game with very low betting limits, mainly for recreational players or players just learning casino style poker. Could be a home game.

Soft break: When a player wants to play less money than the denomination of a bill (usually a $50 or $100 bill), the dealer calls for a "soft break" (part chips and part "soft" or cash).

Soft game: A game with several very weak players, offering good potential for a profit.

Splash the pot: A player who throws chips directly into the pot is said to have "splashed the pot." This is unacceptable because other players cannot see exactly how much was put in.

Split limit: Usually the same as "structured limit" or "fixed limit," but this term may also be used to indicate "mixed limit."

Spread: (1) The range of betting allowed (se also **spread limit.**) (2) To provide a certain game for players, as in "Does the [casino name] spread Omaha?" (See also **dead spread.**)

Spread limit: A limit structure that allows betting any amount within a specified range; e.g., $1 to $4 or $1 to $5 at any time.

Stack: Twenty chips in a stack or column.

Stacking: A method of cheating by arranging the cards in the deck into a desired order to favor a particular player. (See also **mechanic.**)

Stake: (n) The total chips and/or money a player is willing to wager; (v) To loan money to a player, often with the expectation of receiving half of any resulting winnings. (See also **being staked** and **table stakes.**)

Starting requirement: The minimum initial hand a player considers he needs to continue in a pot.

Start the action: (1) The act of a player making the first bet in a particular hand or betting round; (2) The act by the dealer of getting the players to act if they don't start on their own.

Steal: To cause all opponents to fold when a player probably does not have the best hand. The term is used especially in reference to **stealing the antes** — that is, raising on the first round of betting so that everyone remaining in the pot folds.

Steal the antes: See above.

Steal the button: A player in a late position raises, hoping that all following players will fold, thus making himself last to act in subsequent betting rounds. (In effect, he then has the dealer button.)

Stiff: A player who does not toke the dealer. (This derogatory slang term is defined here only to admonish dealers to never utter this word within hearing of any player.)

Straddle: A blind raise before the cards are dealt, posted by the first player after the big blind. A straddle is usually "live," that is, the player posting the straddle has the last option to raise. Usually a straddle must be exactly twice the big blind. Some rooms do not allow a straddle, in which case such a bet would be merely a blind raise. A few rooms may allow a second straddle — but it is not a live blind.

Straight: Any five cards of mixed suits in sequence. For example,

is a straight.

Straight flush: Any five cards of the same suit in sequence. For example,

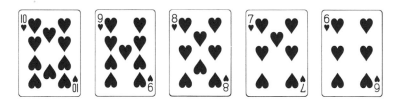

is a straight flush.

Street: The dealing and betting round in a stud game. For example, when each player has received six cards, the action is said to be "on sixth street." Occasionally used in hold 'em or Omaha to indicate how many community cards have been put up. (For example, "fourth street" denotes the fourth board card.)

String bet: The act of putting out a bet in two motions without first stating one's intentions. Since it can be used as a deceitful move it is not allowed in most public cardrooms, so the amount first released determines the size of the bet.

String raise: Like a string bet, this is a raise that is made in two motions or by saying "raise" *after* the call amount has been released in the betting area of the table. Since this can be done as a deceitful move, it is not allowed in public cardrooms. To raise, a player must either say "raise" before releasing any money into the pot or put all of the money for the call and the raise into the pot in one motion (but not an oversize chip or bill with no statement).

Structure: The limits set upon the ante, forced bets, and subsequent bets and raises in any given game.

Structured limit: Betting limits where the amount of any bet or raise is specified for each betting round, and no range of bets is allowed. (See also **fixed limit** and **split limit.**)

Stub: The remainder of the deck after all cards necessary for the current hand have been dealt.

Stuck: Losing money, especially a substantial amount of money, in a given session or over a period of time.

Stud: Poker games in which some of each player's cards are dealt face up.

Sucker: A player who can be expected to lose money, especially one who is not as good as he thinks.

Suit: Clubs, diamonds, hearts, or spades. The suit of a card has no bearing on the value of a hand except to determine whether a flush exists or as might be specified by house rules in certain unusual cases. However, the suit of two cards of the same rank is used to determine the bring-in in seven-card stud. In this case, the deuce of clubs is the lowest and the ace of spades is the highest.

Suited: Two or more cards of the same suit.

Sweeper: Same as a **scooper.**

Table captain: A player who takes it upon himself or herself to direct the action at the table. This is the dealer's job, and the dealer must tactfully retain control of the game.

Table stakes: House policy in nearly all public cardrooms. A player can bet only the money he or she has voluntarily put on the table before the cards are dealt for each hand. A player can not be put at risk for more than that amount and may not take money off the table before leaving the game except to toke the dealer or other service persons. A player may, however, add to his table stake at anytime *between* hands. (See also **side pot** and **all-in.**)

Tap:. (v) To bet or raise an amount equal to an opponent's entire remaining table stake; (n) An incoming dealer taps the seated dealer on the shoulder to let him know he's being pushed

Tap the rack: This is done to notify the table that you are placing a toke in your pocket. Remember, tapping the rack only is *not* an appropriate way to say thank you for a toke. *Always say "Thank you."*

Tap the table: What every dealer will do to alert the players that they are about to burn a card for the next round.

Telephone booth: Same as a **calling station** (slang).

Tell: A habitual move or gesture recognized by another player, thus telling the opponent whether they have a weak or strong hand. (See also **read.**)

Texas hold 'em: A form of poker that uses seven cards — five of which are community board cards, and includes four rounds of betting.

Third Street: In stud games, the third card dealt to each player. (See also **door card.**)

Thirty miles or **thirty days:** Three tens (slang).

Three flush: Three cards of the same suit.

Three-of-a-kind: Three cards of the same rank. For example, three 8s is three-of-a-kind.

Tight: Playing fewer hands than the typical player.

Tilt: See **on tilt.**

Time: (1) An announcement by a player requesting more time to make a decision or by the dealer to prevent out of turn action; (2) A per-player charge taken periodically (e.g., every half hour) rather than raking each pot.

Toke: A gratuity given to the dealer, usually by the winner of a pot.

Top pair: Making a pair by having a card in one's hand of the same rank as the highest ranked card on the board.

Topping: A method of cheating by placing a palmed card on top of the deck. (To avoid suspicion, always follow proper dealing procedure by never covering the deck or otherwise obscuring it from the players' view.)

Trey: A card of rank three. There are no "threes" in a poker deck, always treys. (See also **crab.**)

Trips: Three of a kind (slang) (See also **set.**)

Turn: To deal any card face up.

Turn card: (1) The fourth card in seven-card stud; (2) The fourth board card in hold 'em or Omaha; (3) Sometime used to refer to the flop in hold 'em.

Two: Be careful how you use this word. "Deuce" is the preferred term for a card with two pips, and two cards of the same rank are referred to as a pair. Also, announce a $2 bet (or a $200 bet) simply as "two" or "two to call."

Two flush: Two cards of the same suit.

Underdog: In poker, before all the cards are out, a hand that does not have the best chance of winning.

Underpair: A pocket pair that is lower than any card on the board (or perhaps just lower than the highest card on the board).

Under the gun: The first person to act on the first round of betting is under the gun. On later betting rounds, the player to the immediate left of the bettor is said to be under the gun.

Up: Expressions like aces-up, kings-up, and sixes-up mean two pair with two aces, two kings, or two sixes as the highest of the two pair. Unless an opponent has a top pair of the same rank, the rank of the second pair is of no importance.

Up card: A card that is dealt face up.

Up dealer: A dealer who is on break. (He may be next to push the line.)

VIP or V.I.P.: A Very Important Person; i.e., a preferred customer. Usually a high roller.

Wager: A bet.

Wash: Same as **scramble**.

Well: The portion of the dealer's rack that holds the spare deck of cards and any cash that's in the rack.

Wheel: See **bicycle**.

Wheel card: Any card rank of ace, deuce, trey, four, or five.

Wild card: A joker or any other card mutually agreed upon by the players in the game which can be used to represent any card needed.

Wired pair: A pair in the hole, especially in stud.

World's fair: A monster hand, perhaps the nuts (slang).

World Series of Poker: An annual series of some fifteen poker tournaments with buy-ins ranging up to $10,000, which is held each spring at the Horseshoe Casino in Las Vegas. The competition is generally recognized as the premier competition among the best poker players in the world.

Index

NOTES

NOTES

NOTES

NOTES